COMICS CAREER

TALES FROM THE TITANS!

Top comics pros
reveal how to create a
career in comic books

Interviews by Kirk Chritton

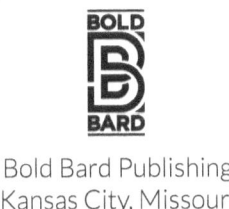

Bold Bard Publishing
Kansas City, Missouri

The contents of this book were originally published in *Comics Career Newsletter*, *Comics Career*, and ComicsCareer.com. Interviews conducted and edited by Kirk Chritton.

ISBN: 9798616762085

*Dedicated to the
comics creators who
sparked my imagination
and illuminated my world.*

Contents

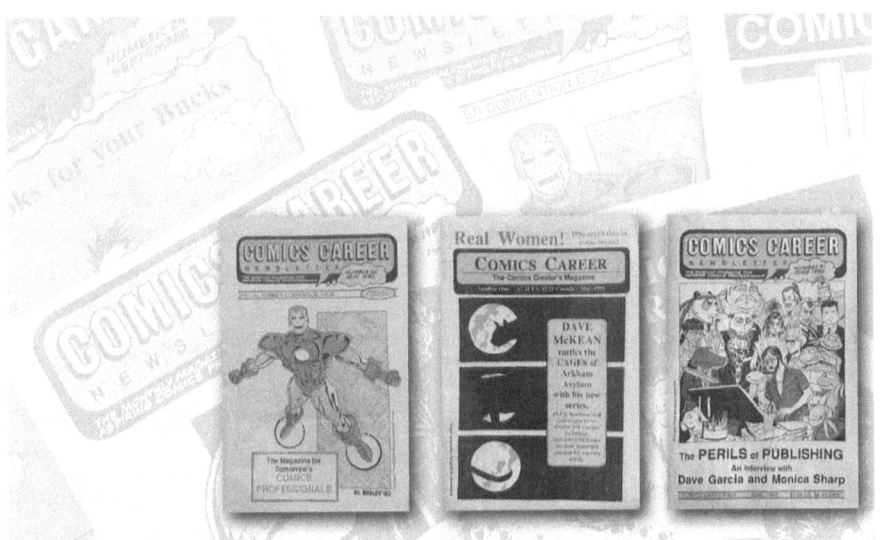

Introduction

I've always been fascinated by the craft of creating comics. In 7th grade, I was scrawling the adventures of my own superheroes on notebook paper. My fandom progressed through photocopied zines, a weekly comic strip in my hometown paper, contributing to professional comics newszines, and finally to a stint as a professional comics writer.

Along the way, I launched *Comics Career Newsletter*, a zine devoted to helping young writers and artists become professional comics creators. CCN ran for 28 issues with an ever-expanding reach. We featured a variety of columnists and articles. Our contributors included established creators like *Superman* writer Paul Kupperberg, Innovation Comics publisher David Campiti, and *Cerebus* creator Dave Sim. The letters column was filled with lively discussion from fans and pros alike. We even received a letter from legendary Golden Age Batman artist Dick Sprang!

After a 14-year gap to raise small children, I returned to the topic. I resurrected the zine for the internet age as ComicsCareer.com in 2008. It continued with articles, interviews, bios, columns, cartoons and more.

One of my personal highlights was conducting in-depth interviews with a variety of comics creators. The interviews weren't promotional pieces. Instead, they were meant to get you inside the process of comics writers, artists, editors, and publishers. The conversations focused on craft and career management. What does it really take to produce professional work? How do creators need to think, feel, and behave to get their first gig? How do they keep getting new assignments?

This book gathers the most powerful and relevant interviews that I conducted for *Comics Career*. They have been lightly edited for clarity and length. I've removed sections that have been eclipsed by changing technology and business practices. What remains are timeless tips and insight from some of the titans of the comic book business.

If you have the spark to create comics, I'm confident that the insights in this book can help shape your own journey.

Kirk Chritton
February 2020

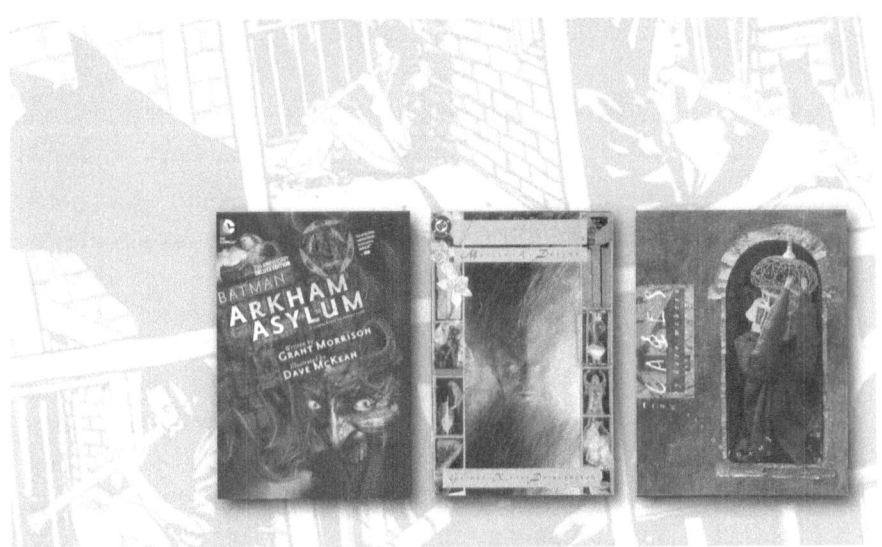

Dave McKean

Dave McKean is an acclaimed illustrator, writer, photographer, and film-maker. His comics work includes his hugely influential work on Arkham Asylum *and dozens of innovate covers for* Sandman *and* Hellblazer.

*Ever exploring new creative horizons, McKean is a prolific but thoughtful creator. In addition to graphic novel collaborations with Neil Gaiman (*Black Orchid, Signal to Noise*) and Grant Morrison (*Arkham Asylum*), he has written graphic novels (*Cages*) and collections of short comics (*Pictures That Tick*), designed sets and projections for the stage (*Lestat*), illustrated children's books (*Coraline, The Graveyard Book, The Day I Swapped My Dad for Two Goldfish*), and directed the feature film* MirrorMask.

This in-depth conversation with Kirk Chritton was conducted upon the initial release of Cages. *In it, he discusses his difficult engaging with superheroes, the differences between US, European, and UK comics, his approach to* Sandman *covers, his use of photo reference, and much more.*

COMICS CAREER: How did you get started with *Cages*?

MCKEAN: It's based on a collection of little ideas I've gathered while working on other writers' projects. Writing ideas are like gold dust. They come along very rarely, so it's taken ages to actually get enough material together—enough things that I wanted to actually put down— to get a book out of it.

I don't really want to go into the plot too much. It's broadly about why people believe in things and what happens when you believe in things. The nature of belief. It's linked to my beliefs. I'm not a religious person, but I believe very strongly in creativity as a force to get you through life. So, it's just about that really, and since it's the first thing I've written, I wanted to stay on home ground and not bite off more than I can chew.

COMICS CAREER: How confident do you feel going into this as a first-time writer?

MCKEAN: I feel reasonably confident now that I'm actually doing it. Up until about four months ago I hadn't got any thing down on paper, so I felt nervous telling the people I talk to, like Neil Gaiman, about it and getting their feedback. It sounded all very grandiose and interesting, but actually putting something on paper was quite different. Now that I've actually got something down, I'm pleased with it, and that was the main thing since I really haven't been all that happy with anything I've done for the last few years.

COMICS CAREER: You haven't been?

MCKEAN: No, not at all. I just really wanted to do something that I was pleased with, something that I could stand up and defend, and be proud of, and show people, and say, "This one's mine."

COMICS CAREER: When you say you're not happy with what you've done, is that in terms of material, doing superhero work, or a feeling that your own artwork wasn't up to par?

MCKEAN: Pretty much everything. I was never happy doing superhero stuff because I've never liked them. And the more I did it, the more I realized that I couldn't do it even as a job. I couldn't get out of bed in the morning—couldn't work up the enthusiasm to do it—because I didn't believe in it. If somebody's doing superhero comics, and they really love it, and it's what they always want to do, fine, more power to them, but not for me.

COMICS CAREER: Was *Arkham Asylum* something of a breaking point?

MCKEAN: It was kind of a breaking point in as much as at the beginning of it. I thought if could push it as far as I could in the direction that I wanted to go—this sort of very abstracted work and dense atmosphere. I tried not to accept any of the ground rules at face value.

When Grant [Morrison] first came up with the story, he didn't know who was going to be drawing it, so it was a very traditional Batman story. But it had Robin in it, and I didn't like that at all. At one point he was Bruce Wayne, and I didn't want that either because I don't believe in the character as a human being. I like the idea of him being sort of a cross between man and an animal, and I think as a mythic story that's kind of interesting.

We chopped it and changed it around.

It became sort of a symbolic play. We piled all this stuff on top of it, and dressed it up in its best clothes, and sent it out. Then I sat down afterwards and realized, "Why? Why bother? It's such an absurd thing to do." It's like suddenly realizing the fact that you're desperately trying to work around the subject matter—trying to make the book despite the subject, rather than because of it At the end of the day, if you really love to do Batman comics, then that's probably the best thing to do. Not liking them, and then trying to make something out of them is just a waste of time.

Also, by the end of it I'd really begun to think that this whole thing about full-color comics with very, very overpainted, lavish illustrations in every panel just didn't work. It hampers the storytelling. It does everything wrong. It's very difficult to have any enthusiasm about it after that.

COMICS CAREER: So, you came to the point that it seemed like the art was working against the story?

MCKEAN: Yeah, definitely. Especially in this case. There was so little content there. I mean, it does nobody any good at all to realize that Batman is a psychopath. Who cares?

COMICS CAREER: There isn't much world-shaking significance in that fact.

MCKEAN: Exactly.

COMICS CAREER: When you say that you realized that full-color, painted work was hampering the story, is that why *Cages* seems to be such a different approach to comics storytelling for you?

MCKEAN: Well, I suppose so. I don't think it is, you see. Because the trouble is—and it's taken seeing other people doing full-color work to make me realize this—what a lot of people are seeing is the surface of what I've been doing. It's all atmosphere and lush colors and texture and this kind of stuff. I've always thought that if there was any strength in my work at all, it was in the basic drawings. Now, I go to conventions and people show me their portfolios and they're full of tons of paint and texture and airbrush and, Christ, it's got bits of watch stuck on it, but the basic drawing is—nine times out of ten—really poor or almost non-existent. So, it was really worrying. I've started to feel responsible for convincing people to just splatter it with paint and forget the drawing.

With *Cages*, I really wanted to do something that was all drawing and as little flash as possible, so it's all pared down to the absolute essential skeleton of the drawing. It's probably still overdone. I think it works a lot better. Just through reading it, you don't stop. There are no false stops. It just keeps you moving through it, I hope, very easily. I've been pleased with the feedback it's been getting. It seems to bear out what I was striving for.

COMICS CAREER: You mentioned that you don't want to do any more superhero work. Does this mean that we'll be seeing you do less work for DC? I've read that you're drawing Jamie Delano's last issue of *Hellblazer*.

MCKEAN: Yeah, I've done that. It should be out soon. That really came about because I've been trying to get together with Jamie to do something for ages—in fact, since I started doing the covers for *Hellblazer* three years ago. He's a good friend, and we wanted to do something, but Jamie—having done three years with Constantine—had got to the end of what he wanted to do with that. Karen [Berger] suggested that I could do the last one, which was nice. Unfortunately, it was a bit rushed, so I didn't have the time to spend that I would have liked.

It's pen and ink, but it's much more cross-hatched and much more tonal pen and ink—if you can have such a thing—than *Cages* is. Then I went over to Ireland and colored it on the computer by hand so that it looks like a full-color thing, but it's kind of a halfway stage.

COMICS CAREER: So, will there still be DC work? Will you keep doing the covers?

MCKEAN: Well, I'll certainly keep doing the *Sandman* covers until somebody throws me off, really, because I love doing them. Apart from the fact I like the comics and like Neil's writing a lot, it's just a great, broad framework of subject matter to go in. He really worked out a little universe there that you can have anybody in. It's really nice to work in such a free world.

But in terms of doing books, I've by no means fallen out with DC. They've been very nice, and I know other people have had problems, but I certainly haven't. Karen's a great editor, and some of the other people there, like Tom Peyer, are really nice. I'd still like to do books for them, but the trouble is if you want to keep on moving forward in any sense, unless you're left alone to grow at your own speed and just do what you feel is right, you're going to eventually hit the ceiling, you're going to hit a wall where you can't go any further. At DC you are very much a hired person; you're working for them. If you want to grow at all, you'll eventually hit the wall. You just have to realize that that's the case, and it won't change. You can try to push the wall a bit and force them to change a little bit, but eventually you'll hit that wall. It just means that you have to look around for other places to do your work.

COMICS CAREER: So, do you see you doing your future work through more individual avenues like Tundra, which is almost a self-publishing situation?

MCKEAN: I think so. Tundra is kind of a dream of a situation. The very loose contracts they've got are absolute dream contracts. They're very nice, personable people to deal with, and you certainly feel like they are working for you inasmuch as they want to try to make the book its very best and that's first on the priority list. Even to have the thing about making money, the profit thing, as being second on the list is an improvement over the obvious first on the list with the big companies.

I don't see that there is anything I'm likely to do that Tundra wouldn't want, unless the quality of it was obviously poor, which is only my fault. And the other place that I'm doing stuff is a book publisher in London called Victor Gollancz. They started as a science fiction book publisher, but now they publish all sorts of different things, and they've just started a line of comics. Again, a good editor, very easy people to work for, and it's a good situation. I'm doing two books for them at the moment.

COMICS CAREER: Will those be distributed in the U.S.?

MCKEAN: They will be distributed in the U.S. We're hoping to work out a deal, possibly even with Tundra. At the moment, they've got two books from me and Neil, Alan Moore, Mike Harrison, and Ian Miller arc all doing comics for them. It's quite a nice little list they've got. And the books that I've seen arc superb.

COMICS CAREER: Here in the U.S. we kind of have this vision of all the British creators sitting in one community controlling our industry and taking away our opportunities. How much contact do you have with the various other creators over there?

MCKEAN: It's exactly like that. We've got a control room! *[Laughter]*

No, we're spread out all over the country. All the different people who are doing American comics are spread out from the top of Scotland and beyond all the way down to the Isle of Wight. It's difficult to stay in touch, or even know everybody. There are certainly quite a few I haven't even met. But we all tend to know each other, and then there are the little groups within that. My immediate friends tend to be Neil and then a few guys like Mark Johnson and Mark Buckingham and Richard Rayner, and a few more established people like John Bolton and Brian Bolland. There are other crowds, like the general *2000 AD.* crowd who I don't really know because I've just never done any work for them. We tend not to see each other.

COMICS CAREER: I think there's a perception over here that there's a very marked stylistic difference between U.S. and British artists and writers. Do you see that, and what do you think the differences are?

MCKEAN: I kind of see the differences. Only talking about Neil, Grant [Morrison], Jamie [Delano], and Alan as writers, because that is generally the work that I look at more than anything else that's produced over here, they tend to just not accept the restrictions. All of them are capable of doing anything they want. Neil has worked as a journalist and has written novels. Grant's written plays. They've all done the work, and they're all capable of doing the work, because at the end of the day, the skills of being a writer are pretty much the same. You have to be able to tell a story. You have to have an ear for dialogue and characterization. It's the same with drawing. Drawing is basic skills. So, if you can do it, you can do anything. Maybe you can do some better than others, but the skills are pretty much the same.

I tend to feel that the skills in American comics have become so specialized that what you actually have to do to write an American superhero comic has become so dictated and constricted that it's not surprising that it tends to be very samey. That's the main stylistic difference. I think the reason it's there is because of two reasons. One is that guys I mentioned are not fans. They're all enthusiastic about comics, and love doing it, and want to keep pushing, but are also extremely critical of comics generally. I know for a fact that for whatever criticism they've got for their respective books, they could write far better criticisms, because they're so critical.

I'm the same way. There are very few comics I like—I can count them on one hand—simply because you almost have to be that critical if you're going to be motivated, if you're going to keep pushing forward. Even when something comes out from somebody you really like, you have to sit down and think, "What is there in here that isn't working? How can you improve on this?" That's a strong motivation.

Plus, the other thing is the geographical part of it It's essentially British stuff. Where in America you've had very much a limited number of genres to work in - it's primarily superheroes and a few other small genres. It's pushed Bill Sienkiewicz, Frank Miller, and a few others to really try to absolutely stretch those thin genres out to their maximums, so it's produced some interesting work because they have to push like crazy to actually get anything interesting. In Europe, they've been able to do anything they want - comics about absolutely anything they fancy doing at all. But, conversely, it's produced a smaller range of styles because the storytelling is often very similar from one European comic to another, although the subject matter is very wide. So, stuck in the middle here, in this little island, we pick and choose from America and Europe, and hopefully come out with something that is the best of both.

COMICS CAREER: You talk about the diversity of the writers, what diversity is there on your part, in terms of a variety of art experience and background? It's obvious that you've done work beyond comics.

MCKEAN: Apart from comics? Well, it's about half and half. I still do tons of illustrations for book covers. In fact, I've just won an award for best album cover of the year.

COMICS CAREER: Congratulations.

MCKEAN: Thank you. I couldn't believe it. I thought they' d made a mistake.

I've done an audio-visual installation for a museum in Carlisle. I've worked as a production designer on a movie in Hollywood for a short while.

COMICS CAREER: What movie was that?

MCKEAN: It was all preproduction work on a movie called *Ecotopia*, and it's all still in preproduction, so you probably won't even hear of it until 1992. I've done music for videos. We're doing a play, a collection of readings by some science fiction authors here, and I'm doing all the music and painting the backdrop and doing some theatre for it. All of that stuff feeds the comics, and all the aspects of comics that you don't get from just sitting down and sketching stuff—like storytelling—feeds the rest. The ability to work with a writer and capture what the writer had in mind in the script obviously feeds into doing an illustration for a book cover because you have to sit down and imagine what the writer would have on his book cover. It all cross feeds.

COMICS CAREER: How does a *Sandman* cover come about? How do you come up with an initial idea and take it to a finished piece? I ask because what you do looks so unlike what other people are doing.

MCKEAN: I talk to Neil pretty much every day. We've got three or four books in the works, so we have to keep abreast of what's going on. What that means is that as soon as Neil has any sort of idea about what's going to be happening in the future as far as the Sandman, he can tell me, and I can start planning it out.

COMICS CAREER: Do you tend to do a series of covers in a row, uninterrupted by other work?

MCKEAN: That's right. I've been tending to get out of Neil as much information as possible about the next four or five covers and then do them as a bulk. One, because it's easier for me to get it done that way, plus, I try to do the stories, such as the current "Season of Mists" storyline, with a particular feel to them. These have a little box of type at the top with the "In which" quote, and the logo is displayed, moved down a bit. And they're all photographically based, somehow, most of them double exposures. Prior that, we had the short stories, ["Dream Country"], and they were all done in that sort of pointillist painting style. And then the one before that had all the shelving down the side.

COMICS CAREER: Early on I was struck by the shelving. The covers were unlike any previous comics that I can think of. I had never seen paintings integrated into three-dimensional objects and then photographed for a comic book cover. What was the impetus behind that?

MCKEAN: At art college I started doing 3-D work and a lot of flat paper collage, which I'm still doing. It's another place to go. If you do one thing over and over again, it tends to lose that spontaneity. It gets boring, and that boredom communicates itself to the viewer as well as to the person who has to draw it all.

The cover of *Cages* #2 is even more 3-D, as is some of the future stuff for Cages. I've been trying to work out ways to use it in the storytelling. I've got one sequence in *Cages* where I've built a small model of a surreal attic, and by illuminating various parts of the attic and taking a photograph just with a pencil torch, it produces storytelling because you have multiple images where the torch moves around illuminating different parts of the attic. So, there's a way that 3-D work can be integrated into comics, and I hope it will work.

COMICS CAREER: How does your workday tend to go? You're obviously juggling a lot of projects at once, so I imagine there's quite a bit of variation.

MCKEAN: I've learned to my cost that if you try to literally keep four or five projects up in the air, generally, your work suffers because you have to bounce from one to another, although variety is certainly nice.

To sit down for two weeks solid and concentrate on one thing—or 20 pages of a comic book—focuses the work a lot more. At the moment, I'm keeping big chunks of my time, like a solid month, to do an issue of *Cages*, and then, because it's bimonthly, I have a month free to do other stuff.

As far as a workday goes, if it's something I've got lined up, I usually get up around midday, which sounds horribly lazy, and sort of putter around and pretend that I don't have to start immediately and then eventually sort of get down to it. And then I work straight through until about five or six in the morning, just because the phone doesn't ring, and there are stupid things on television, and it's dark and quiet, and it's nice. I like working at that time. Even if I try to change to be more in sync with my wife—because she gets up early and we tend to see each other in the corridor as I'm going to bed and she's getting up—it only takes one deadline, and then my time clock is screwed up again. Other than that, I'm driving around, trying to convince people to sell me skulls, asking people to pose in silly costumes.

COMICS CAREER: Do you tend to shoot a lot of your own photos for reference?

MCKEAN: Yeah, again it's something that started at college. I carried on with it because one of the things I don't like about comics generally are these generic characters that you see a lot of the time. I'd just hate to get to the stage where I think I know what a human being looks like, because you only have to look at the people around you to see the infinite variety. You will never know anything.

Even if you've got a few characters under your belt that you can draw, there will always be more. There will always be their postures and facial expressions and their body language, the way the light falls on them, the clothes they wear, the way their clothes hang on them. There's just so much information that if you try to pretend that you know it all, maybe you'll get away with it for a year, but pretty soon it'll become obvious that that's all you know because that's all the information you have.

I take reference photographs just as a way to keep on looking and keep on reminding myself that I don't know everything, that I don't even know a tiny fraction of what's out there. Even if I could draw a picture, say of somebody lighting a cigarette, and then I take a reference photo of somebody and just say, "Light the cigarette," they'll do it in a way that I just wouldn't have expected. There's just that sort of a flick of the wrist or the way they frown a little bit. I just wouldn't have thought of that. That light that illuminates up the face, but really just catches at the neck a bit. All of these little details are more information, and it makes for believable people, and it makes for natural movements and body language which you can empathize with, which all aids in the storytelling.

COMICS CAREER: Many comics seem to be almost drawn from a template, where everything fits a structure and will fit according to certain rules, but if people open their eyes, life is pretty messy.

MCKEAN: Absolutely. There are no straight lines, and books like *How to Draw Comics the Marvel Way* are horribly destructive. Anybody telling you how to draw comics is a nonstarter; you might as well just give up there and then, because that's not *you* doing it, that's a book telling you how to do it. Even if it can give you some interesting advice, a shortcut or two, in a lot of ways, it's better to go around the long way because you'll pick up more information and get more experience.

Most of the people who come up at conventions with the obligatory "How do I get into comics?" question are just getting to the end of school, around fifteen to seventeen years old and wondering what to do and how to get into comics. It must be awfully tempting, drawing away in sketchbooks and looking at a lot of the stuff that gets published and knowing that they can do as well as *that*. They may not be able to do as well as, say, *that over there*, but they can certainly do as well as *that*. They think, "This guy's making a living at this, why can't I? I'll just step in and do that."

I can understand the temptation to do that, but I always tell them to go to art college, even if they're really, really good. Given any amount of time, a week or three years, they'll get bored with it. They'll realize that that's the amount of information they've got, and more importantly, they haven't got the skills you pick up in art college. Because one thing art college teaches you is the skill of how to learn and how to look. A lot of people think you just go to art college to learn how to draw things, whereas the most important things you learn are the basic human skills you to survive. How to observe. How to think through problems. How to solve problems. How to empathize with people. That's the important stuff. Sitting down in a drawing room and drawing potted plants and stuff is important, but it's not as important as that.

Anybody can sit at home and draw a picture of a potted plant, but to actually be surrounded by people with vast experience and a classroom of people who were all the best person in their school and are now suddenly surrounded by people who can draw as well if not better than them. There's that push, that impetus, to get better. And there are always people criticizing you. It's very important to be able to react to that. At the end of the day, if you go through four years of art college and you want to do comics, your comics will be that much richer, that much better, and you'll be ready to go into the industry at a higher level and not have to put up with inking Bouncing Boy for ten years before getting to do anything you really fancy doing.

In many ways, the companies have had it easy for so long because they've had people banging on their door begging to do comics, saying "This is all I want. I'm a huge fan. I just want to do comics. Don't pay me anything. Screw me around. Give me rotten contracts. I'll sell you my kids and everything just for the chance to do some comics." And the publishers say, "Well...okay. We might let you do something," and that's it. You might as well lock the door and throw away the key because there are no other options for you.

As I was saying before, drawing comics is a set of skills like any other set of skills. You can acquire them. You can learn them. To be an illustrator or a fine artist or a sculptor is a basic set of skills that are around abstract things like observation and hand-to-eye coordination and you really have to go through that before trying to take a short cut to do comics. That's why there's such a problem, because the standards are so low, the standards have been accepted as being so low. It's not surprising that people don't take comics seriously. I'm not surprised at all.

COMICS CAREER: Are there things you would like to see happening in the comic book business that aren't happening?

MCKEAN: Well, really I'd just like there to be as big an audience as is necessary to support unusual and individual work. It's as vague as that, really. I don't want huge companies buying in and putting millions of dollars on the table, because that's not what I'm in it for. I don't want to hear any more stories of Spider-Man selling three million copies. I don't want to hear that. All I'd like is for the people who want to do small interesting work, so long as it's good. I'm not asking for a market to support rubbish. I'd like it to be supported intelligently and creatively and for those people to be comfortable and continue to work.

COMICS CAREER: You said earlier that you could count the comics that you really like on one hand. What are those comics?

MCKEAN: I'm very critical of comics because I'm involved in it. I'm critical of films, but I'm much more a sort of patron. I'm quite happy to go down to the cinema and just watch something that's a good time and cheer and clap, as well as watching more stimulating films, something that's more involving. But, in comics, I'm just far more critical. I almost have to be, just to stay ahead and keep thinking about it.

So, *Fires* is really the only one that's come out that I really have no criticism of. It's just a fabulous book. It's a simple story, which I really like, and it treats a very profound subject—man's relationship with the natural world—with a wonderful lightness of touch. It's a very simple statement. I just think that one's terrific.

Oh, and I've just thought of two more that I can't really criticize. One is called *When the Wind Blows*, which is by Raymond Briggs and was made into a full-length animated film recently. One is called *Geoffrey the Tube Train and the Fat Comedian*, and that's by a British comedian called Alexei Sale and drawn by Oscar Zárate, and both of those are just fabulous. I thought *Why I Hate Saturn* was terrific. I think Kyle [Baker]'s a terrific writer. And there are others around.

I enjoyed *Watchmen*, but I'm not sure now that I could sit down now and get the same feelings from it as I did at the time when it was coming out in its twelve parts. For the first time in years, it actually got me waiting for a new comic to come out. Now, looking back on it, it doesn't have the same effect on me. *V for Vendetta* has a better effect on me, oddly enough. There are lots of people who are doing wonderful stuff, but so far the books they're doing I haven't liked that much. I'm probably being harsh saying I could count the books I like on one hand, but I could probably count the ones I've felt worked beautifully on one hand, and certainly the ones that have affected me the ways my favorite films have. There's this tendency to think, "Well, it's only a comic book," and have less expectation of the comic book than you would of *Citizen Kane* or whatever. There have only been a few that I've thought really fulfilled that.

COMICS CAREER: In terms of your own future, to put it crudely, how long will we have you to kick around in the comic book business? Is there going to come a day where you're going to get bored and say, "Nah, this phase is over."

MCKEAN: Well, I certainly feel like I'm in it for the long haul. I've been less certain, but at the moment, I've never been happier with the stuff I'm doing, and I've never been more enthusiastic about comics generally. Everything at the moment is going swimmingly. I've got several books planned, some with other people, some I want to write myself. I seem to have cultivated at least a small group of people who are curious to see what might happen next, which I'm tremendously grateful for and am very pleased about.

Plus, there are lots of people around who, at the moment, are planning or working on some amazing books. I think next year, or even this year, we're going to see some terrific stuff coming out, and that just fires me up even more, gives me even more enthusiasm.

COMICS CAREER: I'm glad to hear it. We want to have you around for a very long time!

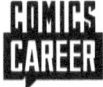

COMICS
CAREER

Dick Giordano

Dick Giordano (1932-2010) was an artist, editor, and executive for DC Comics. In a career that spanned six decades, there was no greater steward of DC's vitality and growth.

In the early '70s, writer Denny O'Neil and the art team of Neal Adams and Giordano redefined Batman as a character driven by his parents' death to stalk the nights fighting crime.

By the '80s, Giordano was leading DC's editorial team. He pushed to open the doors to new approaches to superhero fare including Watchmen *by Alan Moore and Dave Gibbons and* The Dark Knight *by Frank Miller. Giordano led the company's effort to recruit new talent, going so far as to publish a series titled* New Talent Showcase *that was specifically designed to launch young creators.*

I cannot overstate the impact that Dick Giordano had on me during our first meeting. He came to a convention in Kansas City where I watched him interact with creators at his table. He was the ultimate teacher, patiently providing tips to developing artists and pointing out areas to improve. He spoke in the direct but kind tone of a trusted educator. With permission, he would make small marks on artwork or overlay a sheet of paper to sketch out his instructions.

Dick had an insightful understanding of the practical and creative princi-ples of creating comics. In this interview, I recommend paying particular attention to his distinction between being "hired" at a comics company versus having a company as one of your professional clients.

COMICS CAREER: What are some of the basic skills that an artist needs to get an entry level position at DC Comics?

GIORDANO: At least rudimentary knowledge of anatomy and perspec-tive are central after that, the most important thing is storytelling skills. I think you've made a point of that regularly in your magazine, and I say "hurrah" each time. That's really what this is all about. We all serve the needs of the story. This script's the thing. The play's the thing. It's been said eloquently for years; I'm not coming up with a new idea. If you got a good script, then your next job is to get someone who can tell the story as well as it can be told.

Readers are more offended by being confused over something in the storyline and having to re-read it to understand what's happening then they are a by having a nose that's crooked or a mustache that's in the wrong place for the most part, they'll flow right past that if the storytelling is correct.

The whole idea of the artist's role is to give the reader all of the visual information he needs to understand the story. The information given in the graphic backing has to be given by the artist. Any piece that he misses is a mistake. Any piece that he includes is a job well done. If it's drawn well or not isn't as critical as if it's in there and clear. If you know who that person is and what he's doing and where he's doing it, that's storytelling.

If you want to break it down into something that everyone understands, it's the same basics that a newspaper reporter works with in telling his story; who, what, when, where, why. That works very well for comic book artists as well. All those questions have to be answered. Who is this, what he's doing, when he's doing it, where he's doing it, and why he's doing it. It's an effective thing to run through your mind when you are drawing a panel: to make sure all those things are clear to the reader.

COMICS CAREER: What are the basic skills a writer should have?

GIORDANO: I don't know about basic requirements. The thing I'm most concerned with is something we call voice. I don't know how to explain it in simple terms, but I'll try.

Voice is the ability to talk about a theme and the characters who are going to be exploring that theme in the story where you have a clear idea about who the people are by the sound of the voice that the writer creates for them. An example is if you have Batman speak in a panel and there's tail on the balloon and no picture, you still know it's Batman speaking. If a writer can do that, it's a valuable skill.

If a writer can discuss intelligent, mature themes in a way that makes those themes entertaining for his audience, no matter what the age, that's a skill.

We're not interested in plot-driven stories. We're interested in character-driven stories that have themes that can be explored. *Dark Knight* was the exploration of a man growing old and still having a job to do. *Watchmen*'s theme was really what would happen if superheroes really did exist. It has never been explored in that way before. *Green Arrow*, which is my current favorite, explores middle age and the desire to leave something behind. In the past, Green Arrow went around hitting bad guys. That doesn't happen very often in the new Green Arrow book. As a matter of fact, what most concerns Green Arrow is if there's the possibility of having a family with Dinah. It's a theme that's real and that most people can understand to one degree or another.

One of the reasons that Batman has always been so successful is that the origin of Batman was real. No one every really capitalized on that. Everyone can understand watching your parents being murdered as being a motivating factor for turning against crime and for being obsessed with the need to eliminate criminality. It's easy for people to understand that on an emotional level and intellectual level.

We're trying to do more of that. Most of our stories, I hope, will be following the classic literature mode of having the plot being motivated by character, rather than the other way around. In the past, we generally came up with schemes and then found people to put in them. What I'd rather do is explore people, and the storyline will come out of their characterization.

COMICS CAREER: If someone presented DC with a terrific concept, but they don't personally have the skills to do it at that time, what would happen?

GIORDANO: One of two things. We might arrange to buy the concept from them for the proper amount and credit them with the creation. We haven't done that yet, but there's no reason we couldn't. The other one is, if the idea is really that good, I'd have to believe that their ability to execute it would be such that the professionals in the office could influence it to the degree that it would be successful.

I think if someone came up with a great idea, but we believe he can't write it as well as we'd like, we would also believe that we could make the difference. For example, if the writer were a little short, I would probably turn him over to someone like Denny O'Neil. As an editor, Denny is wonderful at instructing writers in structure and storylines so that they can get the most out of their idea.

I think, for example, that Denny has done a wonderful job of getting more out of Cary Bates, who's been a professional writer for years, but then he has spent a little time with Cary to get him to do a little bit more structure in a story. He has also worked with somebody like Mindy Newell, a relative newcomer to the field, and has managed to sharpen her skills to a relatively high level. Andy Helfer is good in that area as well. I would say those are probably the best to work with a writer who has a good idea but isn't able to execute it as well as we'd like.

If it's the artist who has problems, we'd work with other editors. I think Mike Carlin is a little sharper there. I would play a role in some cases where the artwork was close but not right on the money.

Mike Gold is very good at getting people together to get a project done. Each of my editors has very different strengths. We try to use those strengths to our advantage. And to the creator's advantage as often as possible.

COMICS CAREER: Is there something that you're seeing done wrong over and over by aspiring pros?

GIORDANO: I think the major problem is that people who aren't in the business believe that there is some mystery involved in getting into it. One of the things I like about your newsletter is that you try to cut away some of that nonsense and get down to the reality of it. The reality is that it's a business and it's a job. The person who works the hardest is likely to get the best out of it. The person who realizes what he's supposed to do, is likely to achieve the ability to do that.

The only thing I can add to that is my own personal conviction that desire is more important than talent. Whatever "talent" is. I've never been able to define it. But I've seen so many who wanted to do it. And if you really want to do it, you will. Desire is a very, very strong force.

Most of the people who are in comic books today, myself included, got into the industry because it's really what we wanted to do.

COMICS CAREER: How did you get into the business?

GIORDANO: I was sickly as a child and read a lot of comic books. I think everyone who gets into comic books read a lot of them as a kid, and then somewhere along the line found out that they had some of the skill to do part of it and started devoting their life to developing that skill. That's precisely what happened. I read comic books and I enjoyed them a great deal—especially Batman, who's responsible for me being here than anybody else.

One day I was so excited by comic books that I sat down and started drawing and found that I had a limited amount of skill. Like parents are prone to do, my parents thought I was a genius and encouraged me. Fortunately, in grade school, I spent time with my art teacher and mostly did crayon drawings. She thought I had some talent and encouraged me to go to an art vocational high school in New York City. After all that time I spent honing my skill, I decided when I was seven or eight years old that I wanted to be a comic book artist. It was kind of a straight line from that point until I was 19. I never went to college. I entered this industry when I was 19, and I've never done anything else.

COMICS CAREER: What was the first job?

GIORDANO: A one-page filler for Charlton Comics about the Flying Dutchman

COMICS CAREER: And of course, you did a lot of work for Charlton

GIORDANO: Yeah, I started in 1952 on New Year's Day. It made it easy to remember. Actually, I met the editor at someone's house intentionally. My father bird-dogged him for me.

I worked for Charlton fairly steadily through 1967. That makes it 15 years during that time. I also did some work for other publishers, but I always included Charlton as one of my accounts, if not my major account.

From '65 to '67 I was their executive editor and in '67 I moved on to DC and I've pretty much been away from Charlton ever since.

COMICS CAREER: Do you tend to see people's careers running straight lines like that?

GIORDANO: Yeah, pretty much. Today, things are a little harder on newcomers, even though there's a greater demand, because there's no farm system. Charlton was my farm system.

There were some publishers that were the acme of the industry, who paid the most money and had the highest standards and were hardest to get into. At that time, I literally could not bring my samples up to DC. They would not look at them. They didn't need anybody, and they would not come out of the office to look at samples.

But the companies like Charlton—that paid perhaps half the money that DC did—were always looking for new people and were more willing to take chances. My growth was rapid because of working for a company like Charlton. I didn't have any standards to meet, so I could create my own standards for each job. I had very little outside input, except when the job was finished. It's not that I did pencils and then got corrections and then it was inked. I got a script and turned into finished job.

It was a good training system for me, and I don't regret any of it. But there's nothing like that for youngsters coming in today. They basically have to go to a small press and take the chance on getting paid to get practice. Or they have to come to Marvel and DC and knocking on the door, literally, sometimes you get a job. Kevin Maguire walked in the door and two weeks later was doing *Justice League*. I don't recommend you do it that way. But from time to time that someone comes in and is recognized immediately as a formidable new talent and is put to work.

Mostly what you do is keep honing and sharpening your skills. You turn in something for us to look at and we tell you what's wrong with it and you go back and do it again. If you've been listening to me at the table you, you've been hearing me say, "Here's what's wrong, and that's what I want to see an improvement on next time."

They'll hone their skills and after a while they'll be working for the company. It's happened to me maybe 14 or 15 or 16 times where I've been talking to someone at a convention and then a few conventions later, he's working for us. There's a better chance now when we have new a new talent program than say, two years ago, when we weren't looking for anyone specifically

COMICS CAREER: It's wonderful that DC is making such a big investment in new creators. Thank you so much for talking with us.

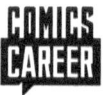

Tom DeFalco

Tom DeFalco served as Marvel Comics' editor-in-chief from 1987 through 1994. In addition to his editorial duties, DeFalco wrote long runs on titles featuring Spider-Man and the Fantastic Four.

He sat down with Comics Career *editor Kirk Chritton for this long interview at a comics convention in 1989. While the roles of various people have changed over the years, DeFalco's comments and advice remain valid.*

COMICS CAREER: Is Marvel usually looking for new talent?

DEFALCO: Marvel is always looking for talent, whether or not this is new talent, meaning this is someone's first job, or this person's just never worked for us before doesn't matter to us. We're always looking for talented people. We don't care where they come from.

COMICS CAREER: Does Marvel currently have some sort of farm system — books that you intentionally use to train your talent?

DEFALCO: Yes, we call it DC Comics. *[Laughter]*

COMICS CAREER: What specific things do you look for in a newcomer's work?

DEFALCO: It is our basic philosophy that people are picking up comic books because they want to read stories. Anything that aids in the reading of a story is a positive thing, and anything that detracts from the story is a negative thing.

When I look at pencils, I check to see if I can follow the whole story visually without words. As far as I'm concerned, the artwork should tell me what's happening and how it's happening. The pencils of the story are essentially a silent movie to me, and if someone can tell a story with only pictures, and tell it in a compelling way, then he's the person we want.

There are some fantastic draftsmen out there, people who draw very beautiful things, but when you look at their pages, what you see is just a series of images which really don't communicate a story. While I can appreciate their draftsmanship a tremendous amount, I don't think that they're right for Marvel.

COMICS CAREER: They're more illustrating pictures from a story than actually telling a story with pictures.

DEFALCO: Yes. Yes. And there are good examples throughout the history of comics. Lou Fine was a fabulous, fabulous illustrator. There are few people who are as good an illustrator as Lou Fine. On the other hand, Jack Kirby is a terrific storyteller. And when you come down to it, I think I'd rather read a comic book by Jack Kirby because I could get into the story, where with Lou Fine I'd just find myself appreciating the beauty of the artwork.

COMICS CAREER: When you're looking at pencils at a convention, do you make a point of not reading the dialogue balloons?

DEFALCO: When someone approaches me with samples, I always ask them "What are you showing me?" What am I supposed to be looking at? The penciling? The inks? Or looking at the balloons because he's a writer? When a guy hands me lettered pages and tells me he's a penciler, I try to only look at the pictures. I consciously try not to read the balloons because I think it's unfair to judge someone on the work of others.

COMICS CAREER: I've heard you talk to several artists here at the convention about overlapping panels. That's something that I see done a lot in comics by flashy artists who play with their panels and build them up over each other. You don't seem to like that. Why is that?

DEFALCO: Because it interferes with the reading of the story. I think a lot of artists do that because they're interested in the design of the page, but people don't read comics a page at a time. They read them a panel at a time.

By designing it for the page, you're really interfering with the reading of the story. Your peers will love it. Art directors around the country will love it. But the reader sitting there will not love it because he won't be drawn into the story the way he should be drawn into the story.

COMICS CAREER: Do you see a movement toward appreciating comics more for the story than for the art?

DEFALCO: I think comics fandom always appreciates the art. I think the pencilers are the true superstars of this industry because the artwork is what makes you buy a comic book the first time. If the writing isn't any good, you will not buy it a second time.

I think also that the art is the most obvious thing. When somebody buys a comic book and likes it, the most obvious thing is the artwork as opposed to the nuances put into the script. Writers are very under appreciated in comic books, but they're under appreciated in most media.

COMICS CAREER: Am I right that Marvel's comics are written almost exclusively plot first? *[Editor's note: This was true in 1989, but not today.]*

DEFALCO: Yeah, I'd say most of them.

COMICS CAREER: But there is a give and take there if the writer prefers to work full script?

DEFALCO: Some writers prefer to work full script, and they work full script. One of our editors prefers storyboards, so his writers work in a storyboard format. It's fairly flexible. It depends on the combination of the writer, the editor, and the penciler. Certain pencilers prefer to work from full script. Other pencilers feel like the looser the plot the better. It just depends on the combination of individuals.

COMICS CAREER: What do you mean by writing a comic book in storyboard format?

DEFALCO: The writer does little sketches, which basically lay out the panel, and puts the balloons in.

COMICS CAREER: Is that difficult for a lot of writers to do?

DEFALCO: If they can't sketch, yes it is!

I worked for Archie Comics, and most of the scripts at that time were in a storyboard format. I created my own lexicon. You could tell who was Archie and who was Jughead and who was Betty and Veronica.

The current editor of Archie, Victor Gorelick, claims that he still has some of those scripts and threatens to blackmail me on occasion. But,

I have friends, Victor, and if any of those scripts surface, you're dead. I know where you live! *[Evil laughter]*

COMICS CAREER: What mistakes do writers make when trying to break in?

DEFALCO: I can't tell you how many people send in—as their first submission—part two of a story when part one just appeared that month. In fact, I've had people send *me* part two to stories where *I* wrote part one. I've already written part two by the time I get their submission. The situations they're resolving are already resolved.

What I suggest to people is to pick a character that they feel sympathetic to, that they have some insight into, and do a story about that character that could appear anytime. A story dealing with themes that are unique to that character and show that character. Most of the Marvel characters are such unique individuals that when you approach them there are such obvious themes that just leap out at you.

When I was doing *Spider-Man* with Ron Frenz ... you know, it's not true that Ron plotted all the stories. I did help him on occasion. I don't remember what that occasion was, but I helped him once. *[Laughter]* But, Ron and I talked on a regular basis to knock out ideas. We had so many ideas for *Spider-Man*, we couldn't produce the book fast enough. There are so many ideas based around those characters that Ron and I were constantly frustrated that we were only capable of doing one monthly book. We were trying to get to the point that we could handle two Spider-Man books, but we just had too many things going on.

COMICS CAREER: You're not really looking for newcomers to give you ideas, because you have plenty of ideas already, right? You're looking for talented people to do something with the ideas.

DEFALCO: Sure. Ideas are cheap, very cheap. In one issue of a comic book you burn up more ideas than you would in an hour of television. It's not so much the basic idea; it's how you handle that idea, the insights you have into that idea, the insights you have into the character. An example I often give is "a teenager gets insect-like powers." Is this a great idea? Well, on the one hand, it was Spider-Man. On the other hand, it was The Fly. Spider-Man became a hit and has been around for years and years and years, while The Fly never got there.

This isn't to say that The Fly is a bad character or that there were bad people on it. It just didn't have the right twists to it.

You can have the same idea done by five different people and four of them will do it in a way that it's a boring, lousy, stupid idea, and one person will turn it into a great masterpiece. There are some people who have the talent to make everything they do turn into gold. Archie Goodwin could write a Milky Way wrapper in such a way that you'd be thrilled and would be waiting to pick up your next candy bar.

COMICS CAREER: In other words, an aspiring writer shouldn't be knocking himself out to come up with a great idea to sell to Marvel, or even one great story, but should be training himself to be someone you can assign to almost any project and turn out quality work.

DEFALCO: He should be training himself, but his initial thing is to do a great story that Marvel would want to buy.

One does not hire writers. One hires secretaries. One hires accountants or window washers, but one does not hire writers. One buys stories from writers.

If you want to be a writer, you have to write those stories. If you write enough good stories, eventually the editors will start chasing you and calling you, and that's the way it works.

I can't tell you how many people come and say, "I'd like to be hired as a writer for Marvel."

My tendency is to say, "Okay, you're hired. You're writing *Fantastic Four*. Give me four plots." And then I'll never hear from those people again.

COMICS CAREER: In other words, you're not the employer of the writer so much as Marvel is the writer's client.

DEFALCO: Yes, and the same with artists.

I'll tell you, there are certain artists we'd love to have working with us but, for assorted reasons, they're not interested in working for us. There are certain writers we'd love to have working for us, but for certain reasons they're not, and the reasons are varied.

COMICS CAREER: They have other clients.

DEFALCO: They have other clients, other interests, other monetary pressures. All sorts of other reasons. Sometimes a brilliant writer just has no interest in doing a particular character. As a writer, there have been many times that I have been offered assignments on various characters that I've had to pass because I just did not feel that I could do the right work for that particular character.

Here's something writers should think about, and this is something I see a lot in submissions. The story is preordained. The villain pops up, the hero pops up, the hero must defeat the villain and does. In the course of the story, the hero is offered no choices. There's only one way he can progress, and of course he always progresses the right way. That is not a story.

COMICS CAREER: A hero would have to be pretty dumb to screw that up.

DEFALCO: Yeah, anyone would have to be dumb to screw it up. That's not a story. Stories deal with people in conflict, and in the course of any story, a character should be making decisions.

You and I are standing here at a convention and we suddenly look across the floor and see a $20 bill laying there. You look at it, see a gentleman standing next to it, and say, "Hey, there's a $20 bill laying there." I look at it and make a dive for it. The guy sees it and tries to put his foot over it. By the different decisions the three of us have made, it shows something about our characters, and that's the important thing that writers have to realize. Characters must make decisions. They have to make choices. If they have no choice, they're not a character; they're a robot! A computer could have done that.

COMICS CAREER: A decision is where the danger lies.

DEFALCO: But, it could be an emotional danger or an intellectual danger. Speaking from my own past, there are certain physical dangers that I have faced and certain emotional dangers I have faced and I'm not so sure which ones were the scariest.

I hate to use my own work as an example, but there was a Spider-Man story where Peter's aunt had asked him to look out for her boyfriend, Nathan, because Nathan was in danger. So, Spider-Man was following Nathan, knowing the man was in danger, and then he heard gunshots and people screaming and had to decide whether to stay with Nathan or go to the other people who were in more immediate danger, and he made a choice. He went to help the other people, and as a result, Nathan was beat up, almost crippled, and sent back to the hospital. It's not a question of guilt. Spider-Man made a choice. He had to go in a direction, weighing the life that's not quite in danger against the life that is in danger.

Sometimes you put people in situations where there is no right decision. I can tell you, many times I've been put into situations where I had two or three choices to make, and I knew that each one of them was wrong because it would cause someone pain and suffering. I had to choose which decision to make. Sometimes in one of those situations you decide you're not going to make a choice, and that in itself is a choice. The thing that separates us from the animals is our ability to make decisions and choices.

I've gotten too philosophical for you, haven't I?

COMICS CAREER: *[Joking]* Yeah, people will think this is too deep for comics.

DEFALCO: This isn't too deep for comics! Nothing is too deep for comics. No subject is beyond comics. No level of sophistication is beyond comics, but when you're talking about mature readers material, I define sophistication by the sophistication of the ideas. Not by the amount of nudity in the comic book. Not by the amount of violence in the comic book. It's the ideas. It's the ideas that can really hurt you, and they can really help you. Our minds are the most powerful weapons we have.

We want, and I want, comic books for all ages, for all people. I think that a lot of the comics that are masquerading as mature reader material are actually very, very sophomoric. I'm not looking to do sophomoric parodies of mature reader material. However, I am trying to do adult comic books. Comics that can stimulate adult imaginations. I'm also trying to do comics for the youngest children. I don't think we've even scratched the surface of what this medium can be.

Right now, the boundaries of what comics can be are so far out there that we can just keep expanding and doing other things and increase the audience. We're doing black and white magazines now like *The Destroyer*. The reason is that we can use characters that are popular in other media and have other fans. By doing comics about these characters, I think we can get other people reading comics. We're doing a book called *Yuppies From Hell.* This is a book drawn by a lady for other ladies in the 25- to 35-year-old category. Single women, out on their own, who are not comic book fans. Yes, we're producing a comic book for people who don't read comics. Why? Because we think that if we produce it we might get them to read comics.

Comic book fans are very paranoid. They think they are unique unto the world, that no one else likes comics except for hardcore comic book fans. *It's a lie!* The second most popular feature in newspapers is the comic strips. Check the bestseller lists. Routinely, there are two or three books of comics: *Garfield, Calvin and Hobbes, Shoe.* Comics and books, comics and books, *comicsandbooks* — keep saying it fast and you'll get another version of comic books! There are comic book readers out there buying vast quantities of comic books, just other types of comic books. We just have to reach out to all fans in different ways.

Talk to people and mention that you really like comics and they'll say, "Man, I really love *Little Orphan Annie,*" or "I can't wait to get to the newspaper to read my favorite strip." Most people really love comics. What's not to love? It's entertainment in it's pure form.

COMICS CAREER: We've talked quite a bit about what you don't want to see from writers. Perhaps you'll tell about what you don't want to see from pencilers.

DEFALCO: I'd prefer to tell you what I do want to see. From pencilers, I want comic book pages. I want to see a few pages showing people in movement and action, doing things. Now, movement and action doesn't necessarily mean punching and hitting. You can show someone bursting through a wall. You can also show someone picking up a tea cup, someone dialing a phone, sitting on a chair, placing a banana peel under someone else's foot.

I like to see backgrounds to see that you can put a figure in a reality. Many times we get portfolios from people of trees and plants and animals and they say, "I do great trees and plants and animals. Hire me as a Marvel Comics artist." But, they don't show us comic book work. If you want to do comic book work, show us comic book work, not advertising pieces.

COMICS CAREER: How about inkers?

DEFALCO: Send us a copy of the penciled page and the inked page. Inking is not tracing the lines. The inker is the final arbiter of reality. He is who decides what is real and what is not real. He is the one who ultimately decides where the blacks are placed. Pencilers are a cowardly and superstitious lot. They all believe they are paid by the amount of graphite they put on a page. They shade something one way it looks like black, they shade it another way it looks like a different black, they shade it a third way, it looks like still another black. If an inker goes over it and inks all three of the black areas as black, he has a totally black panel. So, inkers have to make decisions.

Every line that an inker or a penciler puts down must mean something. It has to be a conscious decision. If you do not know what a line means, do not put it down. Don't shade and cross hatch just for the sake of shading and cross hatching. Let it mean something.

COMICS CAREER: I keep trying to encourage aspiring artists to be self-critical and decide if they're really ready before submitting their material, but it's often difficult to explain what to look for. Are there things that signal that the person's not ready?

DEFALCO: They basically have to look at their ability to draw. What I often say is, take your original artwork, pick up a comic book at random, any comic book, and compare it to your own. Look and see if yours is superior, truly superior, to the comic book that you chose at random. If you are, send your artwork. If you're not, keep working until you are.

In a very real sense, when an artist is coming to Marvel for work, he's looking to take another man's job away from him, so he's got to be better than him.

COMICS CAREER: From a writer's point-of-view, I have people sending me stories and asking for a critique of them. I find that extremely difficult to do. Is there some critical way for a writer to look at his own script and see flaws in the writing?

DEFALCO: There are ways because I constantly look at my own work and see the flaws in the writing. The readers see it as soon as it comes out; it takes me a little while longer. I think most writers do. You look at your work and see what went wrong, what didn't quite work. I've never thought of a way to objectify that.

COMICS CAREER: Maybe the best solution is just to go grab a civilian off the street, put your script in his hand and say, "Is this interesting?"

DEFALCO: But the civilian on the street wouldn't know why it's not interesting. It may be interesting, but be a story that's been done ten thousand times before with no new twists. I always look at a story and say, "What is new about this story? What have we never, ever seen before?" If there's nothing in there that's never been seen before, you shouldn't do that story. Every story has to have something different to be worth the price of admission.

COMICS CAREER: Plus the writer has to be paying more attention to characterization than just inserting the villain of the month.

DEFALCO: The villain of the month is also characterization. Everyone in that book should have his own individual way of approaching the situation. If they don't, the writer has failed.

I can tell you incidents that we've had time and time again. Someone creates a brand new character, and sends in a plot. At one time we actually tried to critique each one, and we'd say, "The character is inconsistent from the beginning of the story to the end of the story."

The creative person says, "That's the way the character is."

We say, "Well, his decisions aren't logical."

He says, "That's the way the character is."

We say, "It doesn't make any sense."

He says, "Well, that's the way the character is."

That's why I don't like to see new characters, because I can't tell if the character is consistent. If someone does a story with Captain America and I look at it, I can tell if they understand the character and how to write a character. If they create their own character, then it's much harder for me to see if it works. In fact, when I get proposals of new characters from new people, even if they've knocked me over with their samples, I just send them back sight unseen. I don't even look at them.

If it's a creative person who has a body of work behind him, that's something else.

Something that most people don't realize is that doing a monthly comic book is a tremendous physical and mental grind. It is a very punishing thing to do your body and mind. Someone who's never done it can't imagine the incredible effort it will take to do it month in and month out. And, to commit to a monthly book is an incredible investment on a company's part. I have to know you can do that.

COMICS CAREER: In other words, you're not interested in buying a monthly book from someone whose track record you don't know.

DEFALCO: No way. Here's the magic of Marvel Comics. If I wanted ten new characters for Monday, Stan Lee is just a phone call away. John Byrne, just dial him up. I have access to some of the greatest talent this industry has ever seen. So, people at home, first learn to walk before you enter a marathon. Take small steps first, and then we'll get you into the marathon.

COMICS CAREER: Are you interested in seeing a progression in a person's work, up from the smaller independent companies?

DEFALCO: I'm only interested in seeing the current work they're doing. When I'm talking about track record, I mean that in terms of committing to a monthly series or that sort of stuff. When someone walks in the door, I don't care if they've done ten monthly books for another company. I want to see what they can do with our characters. The Marvel characters are dramatically different from those of any other company. Anyone who can't see the difference should not even be approaching us for work.

Time and time again I've had people approach me and say, "Yeah, I can do superheroes because they're all the same, blah, blah, blah." Anybody who thinks that should not be doing superheroes, because the difference between characters is so dramatic. We have a weekly assistant editors class. At one point, we took a story that had already been printed. We told the assistant editors to take out the hero in the story and come up with another character and do the same story with the other character. We broke everybody off into small groups, and some groups could not do it, and they were right. Other groups put in another character, and came up with a totally different story, and they were right. One group really tried hard to develop another character and fit him into the story, but realized that it just didn't work with the new character.

COMICS CAREER: How about a little of your background? What's the DeFalco origin story?

DEFALCO: I sprang from the head of Jim Shooter. Fully blown. One day there was nothing there, the next there was an idiot sitting in the office. And, they said, "He is good. We will call him Tom DeFalco." That's it, that's the origin.

COMICS CAREER: Wasn't your first professional comics work for Archie Comics? What roles did you fill there?

DEFALCO: I did a little bit of everything. I started out in their editorial/ production department. I proofread, opened the letters for "Dear Betty and Veronica," pasted up the Archie Club News, did — believe it or not — lettering corrections, coloring corrections.

Archie Comics was, is, and will be an incredible place to start. There are a lot of terrific people there who will go out of their way to help you out and teach you. It was just a fabulous learning ground. And I'm talking about everyone except Victor Gorelick who's trying to black-mail me.

The truth of the matter is that Victor Gorelick, the editor of Archie, is the guy who taught me everything I know. Not everything he knows; I'm still trying to learn it.

COMICS CAREER: But really, Archie comics are a great place to see straight-forward storytelling at its best.

DEFALCO: Sure, but at Archie we would play with the medium in ways that no one else played with the medium. When Marvel does a silent story with no dialogue, it's a big deal, but at Archie, it was routine. At Archie, we told stories in rhyme, in sound effects, in silhouette, or using only the names of the characters. There was no limit to the imagination there.

COMICS CAREER: I just feel like they're underrated by comics fans, as if Archie Comics aren't real comics because they're aimed at a younger age group.

DEFALCO: Sure, but I don't even think they're aimed at a younger age group. I think anybody can appreciate Archie Comics just like anybody can appreciate superhero comics. A lot of comic book fans are locked into what they believe is cool. They unintentionally lock themselves into certain patterns, and it's a shame. There's a wonderful world of comics out there.

COMICS CAREER: There are certainly a lot of people who think Marvel is cool.

DEFALCO: Marvel definitely is cool. And though I'm starting to sound like an ad for Archie Comics, Marvel is the tops in the business. All comic books have pluses and minuses. This is a medium of wonderful potential and wonderful entertainment in so many different ways. Do I sound like a comic book fan?

COMICS CAREER: You sound like a comic book fan.

DEFALCO: I am a big comic book fan!

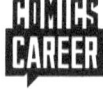

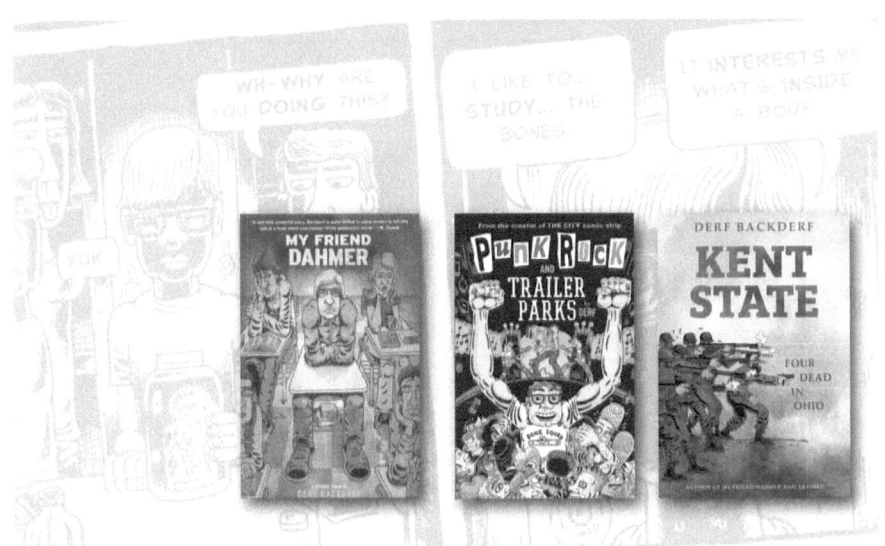

Derf Backderf

John "Derf" Backderf *is a cartoonist and comics creator based in Cleveland. He grew up in Richfield, Ohio, and has turned his formative years into acclaimed graphic novels including* My Friend Dahmer *(2012) and* Trashed *(2015).*

He got his start with his college newspaper and parlayed that experience into a job as a staff artist and editorial cartoonist for daily newspapers. In 1990, he launched a weekly comic strip The City *in alternate newspapers. He self-published early versions of* My Friend Dahmer *and* Trashed.

His graphic novel career skyrocketed with the full-length version of My Friend Dahmer. *That book recounted Derf's high school friendship with future serial killer Jeffrey Dahmer.* Time *magazine named it one of the top five non-fiction books of 2012. It received the Prix Révélation at the 2014 Angoulême International Comics Festival.*

He followed that success with a graphic novel version of Trashed. *His latest graphic novel,* Kent State: Four Dead in Ohio, *will reach bookstores in April 2020.*

This interview was conducted in December 2008 just after the publication of his first full-length graphic novel, Punk Rock and Trailer Parks.

COMICS CAREER: What's the basic premise of *Punk Rock and Trailer Parks*?

DERF: The story, which unfolds in 1980, follows the triumphs and travails of one colorful young man, Otto, who lives in the family-owned trailer park on the outskirts of recession-ravaged Akron, Ohio, the Rubber City. Otto backs into Akron's punk counter-culture, an unlikely and lively punk rock scene that spawned distinctive acts such as Devo, Chrissie Hynde of The Pretenders and so many other groups that *Melody Maker* referred to Akron as "the new Liverpool." By chance and through talent, wit and sheer force of personality, Otto soon becomes a local star. He chases fame and love and has memorable encounters with punk luminaries such as The Clash's Joe Strummer, Wendy O. Williams of The Plasmatics and rock scribe Lester Bangs.

I call it a "rust belt epic." It's a raucous comedy that's as gritty, bawdy and tasteless as punk rock itself.

COMICS CAREER: What makes that era noteworthy to you?

DERF: It was a time of cataclysmic change. That whole Eisenhower-era middle class dream was coming to an end. In the Rust Belt it was just devastation, economic devastation. Some of these towns have never recovered. Akron never recovered.

The best way to demonstrate that is that my dad was a chemist for Goodrich for 35 years. His dad was a foreman at a Goodrich plant for 45 years. My great grandfather was a tire maker at Firestone from the moment he stepped off the boat in 1890 virtually until the day he dropped dead, like 35 years later.

That was not an option for me. When I was coming out of high school, those jobs were gone. And those were good jobs. They were like steel worker jobs, the equivalent of 75 or 80 grand a year. Everyone in town worked at a tire plant. I was the first adult male in my family who didn't.

That resonated throughout the culture. I think it really was a part of the punk rock thing because there were so many kids like me. We were all of that generation where we knew we had to leave town. There were a couple hundred of us who just clustered together in this ratty little club, an abandoned bank, and made this nihilistic caterwaul. We just partied our cares away. It was a perfect setting, sort of a post-apocalyptic scene for this music. I find it to be a really interesting mix of culture, pop culture, politics, and industry.

COMICS CAREER: In that way, I see both the punk rock and the trailer parks in the book as symbolizing that same sort of decline. There's a sense of things that are frayed around the edges.

DERF: Oh, certainly, especially in the Rust Belt and all across the Midwest. And like I said, these towns never recovered. Since I finished it, the book suddenly has this relevancy because of what's going on in the economy now. How much more can we lose? What are these towns going to be like after this round? I shudder to think about it.

COMICS CAREER: How did the idea for the series come about?

DERF: A few years had gone by since my last graphic novel and finally I just decided to sit down and come up with a new book. I was on vacation at a lodge in Canada. Every day, I dragged an Adirondack chair down to the lake and sat there, my feet in the water, a 6-pack of Canadian beer buried in the sand and a sketchpad on my lap. And I wrote from breakfast until sunset for seven straight days. It was fabulous! I had three different concepts I was working on. Otto was one of them.

When I started, I laid out a few goals. First, I wanted this to be fiction, because that's something I hadn't done before. My work to date has either been the absurdist satire of my comic strip, *The City*, or non-fiction, long-form comics. I also wanted this to be a big work, my most ambitious to date. I wanted to return to graphic novels with a bang. I figured, since I made my readers wait so long, I might as well give them a good, long read. And lastly, I was determined to really up the bar as far as the art went. I was going to draw my ass off!

COMICS CAREER: Describe how that creative process played out.

DERF: I came up with Otto right away. He must have been kicking around in my head because he came to me very quickly. And I knew I wanted to have him living in a trailer park. I've always been fascinated with trailer parks. We had one in the small town where I grew up, full of hillbillies from West Virginia who came north to work in the rubber plants in Akron and the trucking depots on the edge of my town. I thought that would be a natural setting where I could work in these other strange characters I had, like the wacko neighbor who barks at people who pass his door and the nymphomaniac bible-thumper and the cantankerous old uncle who drives his lawn tractor around town after he loses his car after too many DUIs.

So I had Otto and the trailer park and several episodes — and that was it. The story was going nowhere. I didn't have any motivation or conflict. I didn't have a plot. So I set it aside and moved on to other projects. But I kept coming back to Otto. There was just something about him that was so attractive.

This struggle with the story went on for the better part of a year. Then I was asked to participate in a benefit concert in Akron, which is 50 miles south of my current Cleveland home, for two musicians from the Rubber City's punk heyday who were having some medical problems. All these old Akron bands were re-forming, some after decades apart, for this show. I drew a poster and the t-shirt for the event. Now I was a first-generation punk rocker, but I wasn't really a part of the then-famous Akron scene — my punk years were spent in other cities — but I always followed the scene and, of course, the music. The benefit was a huge hit. The club was packed, the vibe was tremendous and the bands, though often aged hideously, were phenomenal. It reminded me how great it was. And that's when the brainstorm hit. Of course! I'll put Otto in the Akron punk club!

After that, yeah, I wrote the whole thing in a week. I'm a firm believer in brainstorms. You have to work ideas and that can be a "long, hard slog" but the best work, in my experience, usually comes with some kind of brainstorm, arriving like manna from heaven, complete with a white light and the sound of a heavenly choir — or, in this case, Johnny Ramone and a buzzsaw riff!

COMICS CAREER: Otto definitely has a unique take on life.

DERF: I think he rolls with the punches. I don't think Otto ever really thinks he's going to stick around. He makes a mistake briefly and says he's staying, but he quickly comes to his senses. Otto really represents what a lot of my contemporaries were thinking, and that was, "I'm getting out."

I was so anxious to get out that I started college two weeks after high school graduation. I started summer quarter. Otto really has the same feeling.

COMICS CAREER: Otto is an unusual take on the typical nerd character. How did you approach him?

DERF: The nerd is always a staple of comics, for obvious reasons, and particularly of indie comics. But, he usually seems to be a self-loathing, miserable wretch. The world is pressing down upon him, and "Oh, woe is me." The confessional self-autobiographical comics are particularly prone to this.

I find those characters to be really boring, so when I was thinking about characters, I thought one of the things I haven't seen is the narcissist geek, the egomaniacal geek. We all know people like that. They walk into a room and they just fill it with their sheer force of personality. These are the guys who are running the world now. Bill Gates, Steve Jobs, and all those guys. I thought I should do something like that, because I hadn't seen it before, and I like doing things I haven't seen before. I don't want to cover ground that's been covered. What's the point?

So, that's where I started with Otto. I started building his character, and I found that I really liked what he was becoming. He kind of told me what he was. He just spoke to me off the sketchpad and said, "Put this in and put that in." I just started working with it and piling stuff on. He formed out of thin air on his own, conjured up.

COMICS CAREER: There's a pivotal moment where Otto comes into his own that deals with The Ramones.

DERF: Where Joey takes a big hocker? Yeah, that's actually based on my first Ramones concert. Joey took the biggest loogie I've ever seen. This thing was the size of a baseball. It was amazing.

A lot of the concert stuff I pulled from my own experience at concerts, trying to recreate the same vibe. I've gone to concerts for years and years. I've probably seen the Ramones a dozen times, so I had a lot to pull from.

COMICS CAREER: For a work of fiction, there's a definite sense of verisimilitude to the book. I know people are always asking you if it's autobiographical. How did you bring that sense of "real life" to the book?

DERF: I always write what I know. And what I know is crumbling rust-belt cities and goofy small towns and, yes, punk rock. And when you write what you know, your work, no matter how farcical, will have that element of truth. And that, I think, gives it depth. Those are the things readers respond to.

COMICS CAREER: You've clearly got a handle on the punk rock scene.

DERF: I was a first-generation punk rocker, so this gets back to writing what you know. What I like about punk most of all, outside of great music, is that it remained thoroughly underground throughout the so-called punk era. In fact, there really was no punk era, at least not in this country. In 1980, the charts were dominated by arena rock and disco. The Clash didn't make the Top 100, but Queen, Floyd, Journey and KC and the Sunshine Band were on it for weeks on end! Radio wouldn't play punk. Record stores wouldn't carry it. The media, if it covered punk rock at all, only heaped scorn on it. This was long before the internet. The only way punk spread was by word of mouth. A few dozen enlightened hipsters in every town passing cassette tapes back and forth.

This fascinates me, just as it did back in the day, because it doesn't work like that anymore. The mainstream absorbs the counter-culture almost immediately now. It was great fun to be part of a radical counter-culture. It was dangerous, or felt that way anyway. It was shocking. It was in-your-face. I loved it, especially being a small-town dweeb who, up to that point, was none of those things.

Punk rock gave me an identity, as only music can when you're 19, and a counter-culture aesthetic. I've been feeding off that ever since.

The attraction of punk rock as a theme for the book is that it's something that's retained its "cool" after all these years, probably because it never sold out, or, more accurately, was never given the chance to sell out. The hippies' acid rock was soon converted into elevator music, but punk never made it into the mainstream, not for 20 years anyway. And it's a cultural force that hasn't been examined much, hardly at all in comix. I like telling stories that having been told before.

That's also the reason I set the book in Akron and its punk club, The Bank, and not at CBGBs in New York, which is much more famous. Again, I knew Akron intimately and, although I visited CBGBs, I'd only be guessing what that scene was like. A lot has been written about CBGBs. The Akron scene has been largely forgotten. Again, it's a story that hasn't been told. So it was fun re-creating it and producing what is really the definitive portrait of what it was like.

COMICS CAREER: What was your approach to working the real punk rockers into the story?

DERF: That was the last thing to be added. I didn't want the story to be too Akron. Because who the hell cares about local acts like Unit 5 or Rachel Sweet or Hammer Damage outside of a couple hundred middle-aged scenesters in the Rubber City? So I decided to work in these touring punk luminaries to give the story some star power.

I started by picking some of my personal faves: the Ramones, the Clash, Ian Dury and the Blockheads. And then I added artists that I had seen give memorable performances, such as Klaus Nomi and the Plasmatics. I was two-thirds of the way into it when I noticed that all the people I had chosen were, in fact, no longer with us. So I decided to only use deceased rock stars, partly out of fun and partly to, in some small way, honor them and what they meant to me.

COMICS CAREER: There's a major, unforeseen turn of events at the end of part five which isn't foreshadowed at all. It seems random, but it isn't untrue to the narrative. What inspired you to add that unexpected twist?

DERF: Life is unexpected twists, is it not? In fact, nothing in the story works out the way Otto expects it to. I try not to telegraph anything. I don't think the reader has any idea where this book is going next as they turn the pages. That's something I always enjoy in a book or film.

COMICS CAREER: Your art style in *Punk Rock and Trailer Parks* certainly isn't what a superhero fan would think of as mainstream — it's clearly much more underground influenced. Who are your major influences as an artist and a writer?

DERF: I have inspirations more than I have influences. I'm in awe of people like Robert Crumb and Jack Kirby — but I can't really relate to them, because they are so far above us mere mortals. A guy I really am drawn to is Bill Mauldin, the creator of *Willie and Joe* during World War II and, later, an important political cartoonist. Mauldin wasn't a genius, nor was he blessed with god-like talent — but he is a guy who made the absolute most out of what he had. He is a real inspiration to me.

As a writer, I look outside comics. I think I have a pretty unique voice in my comic strip. Say what you will about it, but there's nothing out there that reads quite the same. I'm proud of that. For longer stories, I mostly look to film and study what works there, because, of course, film and comics share so much. For example, I think *The Big Lebowski* by the Coen Bros is a perfectly written film. That's the gold standard. If I can get within a whiff of something like that, I'm pleased.

COMICS CAREER: How does graphic novel work differ from your comic strip?

DERF: It's a totally different process. The strip is four small panels. It's an absolute. I have to get in, make my point, deliver the punch line and get out. Graphic novels are open-ended. I can make them as long as I want, pace them how I want. It's liberating! I also don't have much room to draw in a comic strip. I did when I started The City and papers ran their strips large. Alas, that is no longer the case. Graphic novels offer that nice, big page and it's totally up to me how to fill them.

The nice thing about a strip, however, is its immediacy. I can draw one in a matter of hours — and a few days later, or even the very next day, there it is in print! I delivered *Punk Rock and Trailer Parks* to SLG in January, and it was almost ten months before it hit the stands. And it was fast-tracked to get it out that soon!

COMICS CAREER: What other projects do you have in the works?

DERF: Nothing definite. I've devoted the last three months to promoting *Punk Rock and Trailer Parks*. Come 2009 and I'll figure out what I'm doing next. I have a few ideas.

COMICS CAREER: When did you first begin creating comics?

DERF: I have comics I drew in the second grade! They ain't bad, either, for a seven-year-old. So it's something I've always done and I don't really have a reason for doing it, other than I love it and always have.

COMICS CAREER: What was life like for seven-year-old Derf?

DERF: My home life growing up was terrific. I had a marvelous childhood, happy and content, growing up in a little town. My adolescence was a little rough, for the usual reasons, and that's when I took solace in comics. My parents never really took an active interest in my artistic endeavors, but they certainly indulged me, buying me whatever supplies I needed. And they supported my career choice without hesitation.

My teachers, on the other hand, largely discouraged me, and occasionally punished me, for drawing comics. I was constantly getting busted for drawing in class when I was in grade school. I actually dropped art altogether in junior high because the fetching hippie art teacher wouldn't let me draw comics. I got a D in art my senior year for drawing too many comics and not enough "real art." Got stiffed on all the scholarships, too. Those went to obedient students who painted pretty watercolor landscapes or still lifes of fruit.

COMICS CAREER: I understand that you were into superhero comics as teenager.

DERF: Yeah, I started with the superhero stuff, Marvel and DC mostly, when I was eight years old. From 1968 to 1978, I was a total comics dork. This was actually kind of a secret shame thing, because high school kids didn't read comics back then. I went to great lengths to keep my addiction hidden from my contemporaries.

As the 70s wore on and mainstream comics got ever more unreadable, I fed my jones by buying Silver Age back issues. They were cheap then. Eventually, I bought up all the back issues I was interested in and that was the end of my comics addiction. By 1981 or so, I was done.

Toward the end I started casting a wider net. I read a lot of the underground stuff; Crumb, Spain, Corben, Bode. But underground comix were wiped out in the early 80s, a victim of, of all things, the war on drugs. This was one of Reagan's first big policy brainstorms, you'll recall. It had — and still has — a negligible effect on the consumption of drugs, but it closed all the head shops almost overnight. And head shops were the main distribution point for underground comix. It would be a few years until the modern comic shops started popping up and the whole indy comics thing started happening, so I was shit out of luck as a comics fan.

It was at that point that I just gave up on comics. I was more interested in music by that time, so my meager discretionary funds were set aside for records and shows. And I really haven't read comics regularly since. I love making comics. Reading them, not so much.

COMICS CAREER: How did your early cartooning work come about?

DERF: I went to the Art Institute of Pittsburgh to learn how to be a comic book artist. It was a huge disappointment. I spent more time learning fashion illustration and how to render motorcycle parts in airbrush than I did on comics. Finally, in my third semester, I got to take a comics and cartooning class. I told the instructor of my dream and he proceeded to shit all over it, telling me what a crappy, low-paying job it was.

"You should draw greeting cards," he advised. "That's a great career!"

I was absolutely crushed. And for some reason, I listened to that guy. Maybe it was because I was so discouraged with what was going on in comic books at the time, I dunno. I gave up the dream and, at the end of the semester, dropped out of art school. It was the only time in my life I've listened to discouraging advice.

So I slunk back home and took the only job I could find, hanging off the back of a garbage truck! Nineteen-year-old college dropout working on a garbage truck in his hometown for minimum wage — how's that for a definition of "loser?" I did that for a year — a miserable, maggot-infested, stinking, reeking year.

Then I returned to school, this time to Ohio State University. I wasn't sure what I was going to major in. That's one of the reasons I chose a big state school. It offered every major under the sun and I planned to figure something out as I went along. Turned out that didn't take long.

Every day at breakfast, I read the school paper, *The Lantern*, and it ran the work of a number of student cartoonists, several strips and a couple who were doing political cartoons. I thought, "I can do this." I picked political cartoons because I think I had some kind of ridiculous delusion that I could use my cartoons to change the world — but I think the main reason was the political cartoons were run bigger than the strips. A couple months later, my first published cartoon appeared in *The Lantern*. And I was on my way.

COMICS CAREER: How did your weekly strip *The City* get started?

DERF: That was a long process. I graduated from Ohio State with a journalism degree and the plan of making it "big" as a political cartoonist. I got a job fairly quickly, as a cartoonist for a small daily in West Palm Beach, FL. It was an okay gig but it didn't take long for me to get restless. The state of political cartooning has been dismal for decades. You can't be overly controversial or provocative. All the cartoons look the same, read the same. Even the lettering is the same! And if you try to break out of that stylistic box, editors freak out. They don't know shit about cartoons, but they're the ones who decide what makes a good cartoon. And it's a real grind, cranking out five cartoons a week. I was really struggling to stay content in the role.

Then, two years in, the paper got a new editor and in a matter of weeks I was fired for, as he put it, "general tastelessness." Bit of a blow at the time, later a badge of honor.

I landed a job as a staff cartoonist-artist with the *Cleveland Plain Dealer*. After that I just kind of wigged out stylistically. I was freed of all the political cartooning restraints. It was two years of intense experimentation with both form and media. I started winning a lot of illustration awards, so the editors left me alone. It was a great period. And I was totally immersed in the counterculture of the late 80s — this was early Gen X — and I drew a lot of inspiration out of that. My work had a relevancy that it had never possessed before.

Eventually, that old itch to make comics returned. The local weekly rag ran a bunch of weird comics, *Life in Hell*, Lynda Barry, Charles Burns, even movie director David Lynch did a strip! And again I thought, "I can do this." So in 1989 I quit my job and holed up in my studio for six months and just drew comics, whatever popped into my head. Eventually I settled on this free-form concept of a cartoon about being a young hipster in a big city. I called it *The City* because, well, that's what it was.

I drew up ten or so strips, mailed copies to this local rag, *The Cleveland Edition*, which was a marvelous paper run by an incredible editor, Bill Gunlocke. He called me the next day and a few weeks later, the strip made its debut. It was an immediate local hit. A year later I started selling it to other similar weeklies. Nineteen years later I'm still doing it.

So it was a seven-year journey from college to *The City*. And I needed every year of that to find my way intellectually and stylistically.

COMICS CAREER: How has your work in *The City* changed over the years?

DERF: When I started off, I was 28 or 29. I was very plugged into the generational politics of the time. This was Gen X and I was doing a lot of stuff based on that. Well, naturally that changes. Ten years later, they're all in the 30s and having kids and leaving that all behind. Then, 9/11 happened and the strip became, I think, much more political. I'm not entirely happy with that, but that's just the way it evolved.

During the last eight years, I think it's been useful. For the first four years, I used to get all kinds of things of threats, and insults, and brickbats from Bush loyalists. It got ugly, especially leading up to the 2004 election. Since then, as Bush has sunk into oblivion, it's really eased up. In fact, I've been doing cartoons lately about that. It's like "Where did everybody go?" It's like they're all hiding under the stairs clutching their George W. Bush action figures and sucking their thumbs. Six years ago they were tattooing the Ten Commandments on the left butt cheek of every third grader, and now they're gone.

There's also been that evolution. You've got to change with the times. I always try to be a contrarian. Now you've got this regime change, and I think we've kind of got to see how it plays out. I think it's going to be tough for me to use it in my writing at first, because I don't know where the material will come from. Here's my point: The strip is always changing, and I sort of let it go.

COMICS CAREER: What were your biggest early influences?

DERF: Probably *MAD* magazine, just like every cartoonist of the past 50 years. I loved — and still love — Don Martin. The rest of the magazine bored me, but I'd plunk down 40 cents for a couple of Martin pieces every month, no problem. And the early guys — Kurtzman, Elder, Wood — I loved them, too. I quickly collected all those paperback reprints.

COMICS CAREER: You talked about writing about what you know. Your teenage interactions with serial killer Jeffrey Dahmer are intriguing. I think to many of us he seems like a fictional character. So many of the things he later did seem beyond comprehension. It has to be different for you. He was a real living, breathing guy you knew as a kid.

DERF: The whole point of *My Friend Dahmer* is that people think of Dahmer or think of Hitler, Mengele, or Osama bin Laden, and they seem like absolute evil. But, you know, they were all kids once. They weren't always evil. It really does a disservice in some way when you just say, "He's pure evil." That's too easy. That's an out. There's a reason they become what they become.

In Dahmer's case, it was this severe dysfunction he had which nobody saw but his contemporaries. All the adults in his life failed him. Every time an adult could have stepped in and said, "Okay, there's something wrong with this kid, let's get him some help," they didn't. That's the real lesson of the book.

And, you see it repeated. With the Columbine kids or the kid at Virgina Tech. It's just the same thing. You can't drop the ball. That was the higher purpose of *My Friend Dahmer*.

COMICS CAREER: What motivated you to put your experiences with him into graphic novel form?

DERF: The motivation was that I had a story to tell. It was a different perspective than anyone else had presented. Here's this guy, and here's what he did. He was actually kind of a tragic figure, which a lot of people have trouble with when they think of Dahmer.

Once he becomes a monster, I lose interest in him. I mean, I'm not a serial killer fan, and God help me, there are people like that out there, and they write me, and they find me. I'm interested in the spiral down. Dahmer came from what should have been an idyllic childhood. Upper middle class. His dad was a chemist. He had a nice house in a beautiful wooded neighborhood. There's no reason he shouldn't have had the type of childhood that I had, which was great. But, he didn't. So you have to think, "Where did that go wrong?" I don't know that there's any clear answer.

The thing about *My Friend Dahmer* is that it's a book that's gotten me a lot of attention, but it's not typical of what I do. So, in that way, it's kind of frustrating. It's so dark and serious, and that's not my usual stuff. Everything else I've done is mostly comedy. So people who discover that book first and then go to my other books, I have the feeling that they're going to be disappointed. It's nowhere near the same.

COMICS CAREER: Did your experiences with Dahmer influence the characters in *Punk Rock and Trailer Parks*? Is there any part of Dahmer's abused loner that reflected into Otto's background?

DERF: No. Nothing. Dahmer's story is dark and dismal. We all well know what the ending is there. Otto's story is a hopeful one. It doesn't turn out like he planned, and there is a tragic element there, but we know great things await Otto.

COMICS CAREER: Turning more to the craft, what's your work routine like?

DERF: For the strip? I usually start thinking about it on Monday, scanning the news, looking for inspiration. I look for punchlines. These typically pop into my head at some point. From the punch line, I write the strip backwards, filling it out. On Wednesdays I sit down and crank out the line art, scan it into Photoshop and add the copy. Then I do a color version. I email everything out — and it all starts again.

Sometimes this process is easy; sometimes it's excruciating. I have a number of partial ideas laying around. Sometimes inspiration will arrive in a flash and I'll figure out how to finish one of these months later.

For comic books, it's a totally different process. I write out the narrative in a small, very rough thumbnail. Mostly I see it in my head, so I don't require a lot of sketch phases, like some creators do. After thumbnails, I go directly to pencils and these are pretty tight. I pencil straight through, page after page, all the way to the end. Then I'll go back and make alterations and corrections, additions or subtractions, and make sure everything is consistent, faces, clothes, that sort of thing. Then I start inking. I use the old pro trick of hopping around all over the book, inking page 5 then page 57 then page 123, so the inking is consistent throughout and doesn't change from front to back.

The books I work on mostly in the evening. I have a laptop drawing board and I park myself on the couch and scribble away while the family watches a DVD. It's a way for me to relax. I chip away at it. The strip, on the other hand, as much as I love doing it, is hard work with a hard deadline.

COMICS CAREER: What drawing tools do you use?

DERF: Mechanical pencils, Micron Pens and Sharpie markers for the blacks. Comics are complicated to compose, but simple to make. That's a great part of their appeal to me, too. Color is added in Photoshop.

COMICS CAREER: Unlike a lot of current comics you seem to do all your lettering by hand. What's your approach to lettering?

DERF: I'm re-thinking that, actually. About a year ago, I switched to computer type for the strip, because papers have shrunk — and in turn reduced the comics — to the point where my hand-lettered type was no longer legible. When I started, the strip typically was stripped across the width of a page, 10 inches or so. I had tons of room to draw and write. These days, I'm lucky if the strip is run half that size. I held out as long as I could, because I like that DIY look. That's a very punk rock stance, too, so I went back to that for *Punk Rock and Trailer Parks* and hand lettered everything. And ya know what? It was a total hassle! It makes corrections and alterations a real pain in the ass. Future books will have computer type.

COMICS CAREER: What is the typical starting point of a story for you?

DERF: Well, I've only the three books — and they all came together differently.

My Friend Dahmer was written for me. It is what it is. The story was there and I can't take credit for it. The struggle was how to put it together and, of course, deal with the story itself, on a personal level. It really fucked with my head, as you can imagine. I started the first chapter of that book about two years after his death. It took five years to finish the rest of the 24-page book!

Trashed, on the other hand, was a complete joy. This too was written for me, because it all really happened, but, unlike *Dahmer*, these were stories I loved to think about and tell people about. I'd been loudly regaling the unwary with tales of maggots and garbage at bars and parties for years, so it was easy to put down on paper. I guess the similarity between the two is that it started with the story.

Punk Rock and Trailer Parks started with Otto. I came up with the character and then wrote the story around him. The difference there is that Otto, by the very nature of him, dictated where that story was going. I could plug him into a situation and that scene would almost write itself.

COMICS CAREER: What has been the most rewarding project?

DERF: *Punk Rock and Trailer Parks* is my baby. It's the most recent, obviously, and I'm very proud of it. I think it's the best thing I've ever done. But I don't think anything will ever top *The City*, especially those first couple years. After years of struggle, I finally produced something that got people talking and taking notice. It was incredibly gratifying.

COMICS CAREER: How do you judge when a story is "done" and you can stop revising it?

DERF: Ha. Usually, it's the deadline that tells me when it's done. I'm a newspaperman at heart and I like working with deadlines. Even if I don't have one, I'll give myself one. There reaches a point with any creator when you just have to let the work go. It'll never be perfect. A deadline helps you let it go.

COMICS CAREER: What advice do you give to others who want to work in the comics industry — either in cartooning or graphic novels?

DERF: The best advice I can give is: find your voice. It has to be yours. And don't worry about failing. It's part of the process.

I learned to cartoon on the pages of the paper at Ohio State. It had a huge daily circulation of 35,000, twice the size of my first pro paper! And it was all students and profs and grad students, smart, educated readers, not some nitwit housewife who gets all her news from religious radio or some bonehead who only reads the paper for the box scores. So I was challenged on my political statements and when I bombed, which was often, it was a very public flame-out. But man! What a great learning experience, under pressure and under fire. For a young cartoonist, I still think that's a great way to go. Find a college with a good school paper.

The future of cartoons, however, is on the web. Concentrate on that. Newspapers and magazines will be gone in 10 years.

As for graphic novels, I wasn't exactly welcomed with open arms into comic books, despite having logged a lot of success with *The City*. I was quite surprised at what a closed little world that is. Both *My Friend Dahmer* and *Trashed* were rejected by every comics publisher in the biz until SLG agreed to publish *Trashed*. And both those books wound up with Eisner nominations!

COMICS CAREER: What are the biggest mistakes you've seen other creators or aspiring professionals make that hurt their chances to advance their careers?

DERF: I think the biggest mistake is giving up too easily. This is not a career for the weak. You can't get discouraged by a few — or a few dozen — rejections.

Comics is a tough business. There's no question. But, if you don't try, you'll never know if you'll be successful or not. I think if you must make comics, you will make comics. There's something there that drives people to do it, and that's how it should be.

Happily, what I've done—which is why I'm swimming in money now—has been a labor of love. I don't make compromises. I do what I want to do in the way I want to do it.

That really sounds noble, but it's really probably fuckin' stupid. *[Laughter]* That's just the way it's always been with me.

COMICS CAREER: The punk rock mentality.

DERF: Well, I guess so. But, y'know, I'd like to make a little more money — no doubt there. Oh well, it's probably too late to worry about that now.

COMICS CAREER: What networking tips have you picked up to promote your work and advance your career?

DERF: Very few, unfortunately! I suck at networking. Which is why I'm the huge success I am today!

COMICS CAREER: At the end of these interviews I tend to get philosophical. How would you sum up the most important "big idea" that you've learned in life, in or out of comics?

DERF: I don't believe in "big ideas." Life is dictated by "little ideas", strung together. Six years ago, I was diagnosed with cancer. I'm fine now, but it was an ordeal: surgery, chemo, radiation, the whole bit. That's why there was a 7-year gap between graphic novels. At the same time, a musician I admire greatly, Warren Zevon, was also battling cancer, a battle he lost. He made one final appearance on David Letterman, who was also a longtime fan. Zevon's prognosis at that point was terminal.

"Is there anything you now know that I don't?" Letterman asked him.

"Enjoy every sandwich," answered Zevon.

That's what I've tried to do ever since, be it ice-skating with my daughter or walking the dog in the woods on a beautiful fall day or producing a strip or book that I'm pleased with.

I have two things hanging over my drawing board. That Zevon quote — and a photo of the garbage truck I worked on so many years ago. One is a reminder of how to live my life — the other a reminder of where I could wind up again if I don't keep working hard.

COMICS CAREER: That's a big inspiration I'm going to look at my next sandwich with a different attitude!

Thanks for the great comics. I'm a big fan. And thank you for talking with me.

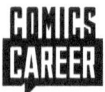

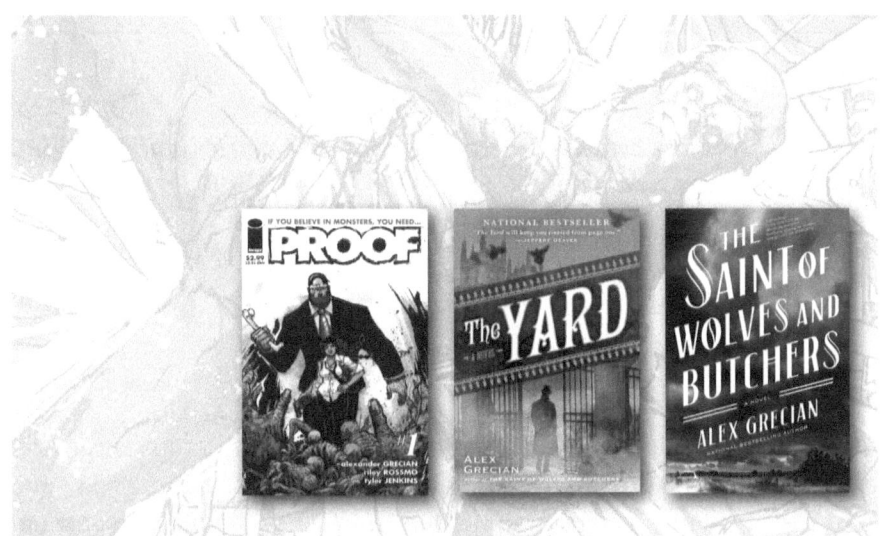

Alex Grecian

From the comics rack to the best-sellers list, Alex Grecian is an acclaimed crime novelist. He started with an interest in writing and drawing comics, eventually deciding to focus on writing. He found success with his creator-owned series Proof *from Image Comics. He balanced writing comics with his initial foray into prose, while also managing quality dad duty.*

I interviewed Alex at a local comics convention and was amazed by his intelligence and versatility—and I didn't even know the full story. He hadn't yet completed the first of his wildly successful crime novels.

His novels are mass market hardcover releases that routinely hit the New York Times Bestsellers list. You'll find them prominently displayed in libraries and airport book stands. The first five books feature Scotland Yard's "murder squad," a group of detectives taking on criminals in the cutthroat alleys of Victorian London. They include The Yard, The Black Country, *and* Lost and Gone Forever. *His most recent release,* The Saint of Wolves and Butchers, *is his first major novel outside the Murder Squad series.*

In this piece, Alex describes his winding career path to comics writ-

ing, the surprising benefits of lettering your own stories, and insightful advice for young creators.

Fun fact: my mother and Alex's uncle used to teach at the same small-town middle school.

COMICS CAREER: Tell us about *Proof.*

GRECIAN: *Proof* is an ongoing series about The Lodge, a top-secret government organization jointly funded by the US and Canada. The Lodge is headed by a mysterious man named Leander Wight whose goal is to ensure that humans and cryptids live in harmony.

Cryptids are monsters that might actually exist, creatures that have been witnessed, but never caught: the Loch Ness Monster, El Chupacabra, the Mothman, Bigfoot,... all cryptids.

Speaking of Bigfoot, The Lodge's star agent is a sasquatch. He's the only non-human agent and he goes by the name John Prufrock. His friends call him Proof for short. He's a stylish guy who cares deeply about his appearance and manners, but for obvious reasons he can't interact with the public.

Proof's partner is Ginger Brown. She was a rookie FBI agent and was recruited by The Lodge after she met a golem while on a case in New York. Other agents include Elvis Chestnut, who came to The Lodge after his mother was killed and inhabited by El Chupacabra; Wayne Russet, Proof's best friend and lead cryptozoologist; and Noel Russet, Wayne's estranged son.

The first story arc *[issues 1-5]* was collected in the *Goatsucker* trade. In it, we're introduced to all these characters, plus an agent named Autumn Song, who isn't terribly nice, but is good at her job. The second arc *[issues 6-9]* is called *The Company Of Men*, and will be collected this

December. That book takes the Lodge agents to Africa in search of a baby dinosaur, then to Seattle to find Elvis a new suit. Currently, Proof is in the American Midwest, dealing with giant thunderbirds.

COMICS CAREER: How did the idea for the series come about?

GRECIAN: A friend of mine made a joke about the reason why nobody's found Bigfoot: The CIA already found him and he's working under-cover. It didn't sound like a joke to me. It sounded like a great idea for a story. As I began to explore what Bigfoot would want and why and how he'd work for the government, the idea took shape, layering over itself like a pearl.

COMICS CAREER: How did you connect with artist Riley Rossmo? What added elements has Riley brought to the series?

GRECIAN: Riley and I did a graphic novel called *Seven Sons* for AiT/Planet Lar and enjoyed working together. When we finished *Seven Sons*, we started casting about for something else to collaborate on. As soon as I started thinking about *Proof*—and long before I had a title for the series—he was the first and only artist who came to mind. Fortunately, he immediately saw as much potential in the idea as I did.

To make a series like *Proof* remotely believable, as opposed to cartoony and silly, the characters need to seem like real people. Or as real as a comic book about Bigfoot can get. Riley's work stands out in many ways, but the thing I like most is his ability to convey facial expressions and body language in a way that allows the characters to communicate without dialogue. That makes my job much easier. He really breathes life into Proof and the supporting cast.

Plus, he's impossibly fast!

COMICS CAREER: Over the first dozen or so issues of *Proof*, have you found that the series has diverged from your original plans?

GRECIAN: In some ways. We started out with a rough blueprint for the entire series and that's still intact. The ending for the series will still be what it's always been. But we went in with a lot of wiggle room to explore things along the way and that's allowed us to have fun and discover aspects of the characters and situations we didn't anticipate.

COMICS CAREER: What surprises have come up along the way?

GRECIAN: There've been a couple of characters who were supposed to die or disappear and they've come back. Elvis Chestnut in particular took on a life of his own and has become integral to the resolution of the entire series. Originally, he was going to be eaten by the chupacabra in issue two. The final issue of *Proof*, though, would be much less satisfying without him, so I'm glad he'll be around to contribute to it.

COMICS CAREER: How does your screenwriting and prose work affect your comics work?

GRECIAN: They're night and day, really. Writing for comic books is much more difficult and restrictive than, say, writing novels or short stories. At least for me. My tendency is to want to explore every avenue that presents itself with a character and you have that freedom when you're writing a novel. As long as the structure is sound, you really don't have to worry about how many pages are in a chapter. But in comics, you're constantly watching the pace, making sure you can fit everything you need in those 22 pages for an issue. Plus, each page is like a chapter, where you've got to be aware of your beats and have a mini-beat fall at the end of the page, prompting the reader to turn to the next page. It's much more challenging for me and a reason I think a lot of novelists don't do well when they make the transition to comics. Of course, many do, but some are probably turned away by the demands of the medium.

The upside, though, is the collaboration. If I'm working with a really good artist, someone like Riley, I get to see the story filtered through him and that gives everything a new dimension it wouldn't otherwise have. I love it.

I've only written one movie treatment and hated every minute of it. That was an adaptation I was asked to write by a production studio and the source material was a terrible comic book series. I agreed to do it before I read the comic and then my heart sank once I actually got the thing and started taking notes. I'd like to take another stab at a screenplay one of these days, writing an original story or adapting something of my own. But the challenges there are tenfold what they are in comics. If you're not careful, I think the story can take a backseat to the demands of the medium and you get kind of lost.

For now, I'm really happy writing comics and crime novels.

COMICS CAREER: Do they cross-pollinate in some fashion?

GRECIAN: Each kind of rejuvenates my creative batteries because I'm exercising different muscles. But writing novels taught me to sit down and write at the same time every day and set a goal for myself. That's become my routine and without it I wouldn't be able to get much done.

COMICS CAREER: I think it's interesting that you're also the book's letterer. As a writer, what are the benefits of having that level of control on the placement of your words?

GRECIAN: Oh, it's enormous, really. It's helped us to remain on-schedule, for starters. I don't have to sweat the dialogue too much, so Riley never ends up waiting on me for scripts. The script I send Riley is pretty detailed, but I don't take the time to go back and choose the words in the dialogue, write another draft of it. Once I get the art back from Riley, I can make my tweaks and reposition things to match the art and help the flow and pacing. That's also the point at which I realize *Proof* wouldn't have phrased a certain sentence the way I first wrote it, etc. I love being able to have that one last swipe at things before it all goes off to the printer, a final draft on the page. I do hate doing the sound effects, though. I cheat on those quite a bit.

COMICS CAREER: I understand that you also create fonts. That's an unusual sideline for a writer. How did your typography work come about?

GRECIAN: I became fascinated with fonts when I worked as a pager— that's someone who lays out publications—for a printer-publisher. They had hundreds, maybe thousands, of fonts on their servers because each magazine they published used a different set of type-faces. But there was no organization to any of it, so in my spare time I put together a font library for them, consolidating everything and learning a lot about fonts as I went along. They used a program called Fontographer to fix damaged fonts and I gradually taught myself how to use that software to make all-new fonts. That eventually turned into a sideline for me.

COMICS CAREER: How has your background in advertising affected your comics career?

GRECIAN: I started as an illustrator and idea guy. I was headhunted after doing freelance work while I still worked for the printer-publisher. I was a busy guy. From there, I was able to move into just about every aspect of ad work, except sales and media buying. I wrote copy, gave presentations, and managed to work my way into directing TV spots. My primary function, though, was to brainstorm new campaigns for clients.

Learning to storyboard for TV and hit deadlines definitely helped me think visually and put a book out on time every month. It was incredibly useful training.

COMICS CAREER: What made you decide to write full time?

GRECIAN: Well, I started to hate my job. The country was going through a recession and about half of my co-workers at the agency were laid off. The atmosphere became extremely political and onerous. I was also stupid enough to sign a non-compete contract when I started there that specifically kept me from doing comic book work. At first that wasn't so bad because I was so busy I didn't have time to even think about comics. But the less happy I was at my day job, the more I wanted to write my own stories as a creative outlet.

When my wife got pregnant, we both wanted our son to have a stay-at-home parent. My wife had a better-paying job, I hated my job, and it seemed logical that I could freelance from home.

The original plan was for me to be a freelance advertising illustrator. But I started writing comic book pitches and scripts and before we knew it I was working full-time to break into comics as a writer. I guess I just finally decided I wasn't going to have any more opportunities to follow my dream. And I was awfully lucky to have such a supportive spouse.

COMICS CAREER: How did your early work in *The Factor*, *24 Hour Comics*, and *Seven Sons* come about? What did you learn from those projects?

GRECIAN: I was introduced to Nat Gertler at a convention when he was looking for artists. I had a portfolio because I was drawing my own stories and he invited me to draw a couple of projects for him, including *The Factor* and *Licensable Bear*. I also wrote and drew a 24-Hour comic, somewhere in there, and turned it into a mini-comic, which I sent around to creators and publications. *CBG* gave it a glowing review and for a while it looked like I had a shot at breaking into comics. But, then I went to work for the agency that wouldn't let me do comics work.

When Nat put together the first *24 Hour Comics* book — which was edited by Scott McCloud and included stories by Neil Gaiman and Stephen Bissette — I was fortunate to have Scott choose my story for inclusion. That encouraged me to go after comics work again.

Mostly what I learned from those projects was that I shouldn't draw. And if you're trying to carve out a career, you shouldn't lose your forward momentum. By disappearing entirely for a five-year period, I ended up having to start all over again.

Seven Sons was a different deal altogether and came much later, after I quit the agency. I decided I really didn't have the chops to draw comics and should just stick to writing. I'd met Riley Rossmo and sent him a list of, I think, 16 story ideas. He picked *Seven Sons* and we put together the graphic novel together, which we sold to the first publisher we approached: AiT. We kept our momentum and used *Seven Sons* to help us sell *Proof* to Image.

COMICS CAREER: Nat Gertler seems to have had a major impact on your early career. Tell me about his influence, and others who have had an important role in your development.

GRECIAN: Nat's a great guy and was very good to me. It was useful to draw from someone else's script because I learned some of the fundamentals of formatting. But I chafed at having to draw someone else's stories and basically figured out the hard way that drawing wasn't the part of the process that I liked. Poor Nat didn't get my best work. I really wanted to be doing what he was doing, not what I was doing.

I was lucky, early on, to have a number of people who encouraged me and gave me confidence. Batton Lash, who writes and draws *Supernat-*

ural Law, and his wife, Jackie Estrada, who runs the Eisner Awards, were terrific. They saw some potential in me, I guess, and introduced me to lots of other comics folks. My wife and I even stayed in their home on our honeymoon! Ande Parks and Phil Hester gave me tons of advice and some early opportunities. My first published work was as an uncredited inking assistant on a Caliber book Ande inked. Paul Fricke, who co-created *Trollords* and inked a ton of DC stuff, was also a great source of advice and became a good friend. Dave Sim and Eddie Campbell also took time to talk and write to me and help me figure things out when I was just starting out. And Brian Wood actually gave Riley and me the introduction to Image that led to us pitching *Proof*.

This industry's full of generous people. Networking's important in just about any field, but it's probably easier in comics because there are so many gifted people who are willing to share their time and knowledge.

COMICS CAREER: When did you first begin creating comics?

GRECIAN: I can't remember. My son's been drawing his own comics since he was two, so I imagine I started at about the same time.

COMICS CAREER: What was your family situation at the time, and did that affect your interests in comics?

GRECIAN: My dad's always read comic books. One of my earliest comic book memories was sitting at the dining room table, reading my dad's copies of the Warren *Spirit* reprints. So, yeah, having comics around and having a parent who's a professional writer, I guess it's not hard to put two and two together.

COMICS CAREER: What were your biggest early influences?

GRECIAN: The first comic I can remember picking apart and examining to see how the creator did what he did was *The Spirit*. Eisner was, and is, a huge influence. *Peanuts* was a big deal for me too.

Probably the most influential early comic for me, though, was an issue of DC's *Showcase* that heralded the "new" Doom Patrol. I'd never heard of the Doom Patrol before, but it was clear that it was a team that'd been around since long before I was born. And the whole team (with the sole exception of Robotman) got killed in that issue. Here I'd just found out about these weird characters and they were suddenly gone. That was huge for me. The idea not just that comic book characters were mortal, but that continuity could move forward and things could change. That's an exciting idea.

And it may be why I still have a tendency to kill off characters as soon as I start to get attached to them. Riley has saved several *Proof* characters from certain death.

COMICS CAREER: From where do you currently draw your inspiration? What do you do to recharge your creative batteries?

GRECIAN: Personally, I like to write in more than one medium to keep things fresh. I'm desperately trying to carve out some time to finish my third crime novel, which I think is the most ambitious project I've ever written.

COMICS CAREER: Ambitious in what way?

GRECIAN: When comic book writers try their hand at writing prose, they tend, at least in my opinion, to overcompensate for the lack of pictures and end up writing horrible, flowery stuff. Neil Gaiman's an exception, of course, and I'm sure there are others. But the two media exercise completely different creative muscles and that takes some adjustment.

Anyway, my first prose novel was kind of a mess and I put it away. It'll never see the light of day. The next two I wrote were much better, I think, leaner and more focused. I'm really proud of them. This third—or fourth, depending on how we count them—is written in the first person, which is trickier than third person perspective, and it's much darker and more serious. I'm trying to tackle some big issues, within the context of a detective novel. Hopefully I'm able to pull it off, but working on it is honestly exhilarating.

COMICS CAREER: What is it about comics that appeals to you as a creator?

GRECIAN: Writing a book is a solitary experience. So is writing a comic book script, but then someone else takes that script and turns it into something else. I guess I love the collaboration more than anything. And that really doesn't apply to writing. I have no interest in collaborating with another writer. I like seeing my work taken to another level through the process of transforming it into another art form.

COMICS CAREER: What's your typical writing routine?

GRECIAN: I get up between five and five-thirty every morning, seven days a week. I drink a pot of coffee while I read and respond to email, check the *Proof* message board and catch up on the day's news. Then I get to my desk before the sun's up and start writing. I usually leave off between scenes so that I can think over the next day's scenes later in the day when I'm not writing.

My wife comes down a little after seven and I send her off to work then get my son up and ready for school. After I take him and get back home, I eat breakfast and then get back to work. In the afternoon, I do production work, color-correcting *Proof* pages, writing letters and pitches, lettering and putting together back-matter. Then I pick my son up from school and I'm just dad, taking care of him and making dinner. It's a nice routine.

I try to pattern my life after the main character, a writer, in *The World*

According to Garp. That was my favorite novel for a long time and another big influence on me.

COMICS CAREER: What is the typical starting point of a story for you?

GRECIAN: The vast majority of my writing time is spent trying to fig-ure out where to begin and end scenes and massaging the transitions between scenes. Every scene starts for me with the characters think-ing about what they want and what they're trying to get accomplished in that scene. The characters are always the starting point. In fact, I began my third novel with no plot and no idea where I was going, just the relationship between two brothers, one of whom is learning dis-abled, and the detective agency they inherited from their father. I love exploring what makes people tick.

COMICS CAREER: How do you judge when a story is "done" and you can stop revising it?

GRECIAN: When Riley calls and says he needs more script pages. *[Laugh-ter]*

COMICS CAREER: What's the most common advice you give to others who want to work in the comics industry?

GRECIAN: It might be presumptuous for me to give advice at this point in my career—but since you asked—I've got a long two-part answer, but it really all boils down to a single word: write!

I think too many aspiring writers give too much weight to ideas. They treat ideas with reverence. An idea is just the first step in a story. And the easiest step. It's a tool to get you into the process. If you want to write, you've got to get your hands dirty and actually write.

An aspiring writer came up to my table at a recent con and asked for some advice. He'd spent years working out his epic comic book series and he was stuck. It sounded like he'd been stuck for a while and he wanted to know how to break past whatever roadblock he'd run into so he could keep going with his masterpiece. My advice to him, which he clearly didn't appreciate, was that he should abandon it and move on to another story.

Since *Proof* started up, I've had a fair number of people email me with this same problem and I always say the same thing. Being a writer is about writing. Yes, absolutely, you've got to work through story problems. But if your story is growing barnacles instead of actually moving forward, then you're not writing, you're just mulling something over.

It's much easier to build an epic in your head than it is to sit down and build individual scenes and characters. But without those things, you don't have a story.

And if you've only got one story to pitch to companies, your chances of breaking in aren't swell. I spent three years writing at least one new pitch a week before a single one of them was picked up by a publisher. Some of those were pretty good, but they didn't meet the editorial needs of the publishers I sent them to and they were rejected. If I'd put all my eggs in one epic basket, I'd still be spinning my wheels now.

The second part of my answer ties into the first. You've got to sit down at a specific time every day and write something. If you're stuck at some point in your masterpiece, you're not gonna get much actual writing done. After a few days of that, you're probably not gonna bother to sit down at your computer or your typewriter or your yellow legal pad. And if you're not writing, you're not a writer, are you?

When I write a novel, I set a daily goal of 2,000 words. When I write a comic book script, I aim for two complete scenes a day, however long those may be. I don't always reach those goals, but there have been days in which I've exceeded them, so I know it's possible. There've also been days in which everything I've written has been worthless, but it's important to sit down and do the work. You can revise or trash your day's work later.

Writing's a job and I think you have to treat it like one. If you sit around and wait for your muse, she may not show up. You've got to force her to show up by sitting and typing or writing longhand, if that's your preference.

COMICS CAREER: What are the biggest mistakes you've seen aspiring professionals make that hurt their chances to advance their careers?

GRECIAN: I'm really going to come across as arrogant when I attempt to answer this. Hopefully I don't completely disappear after I shell out advice about other folks' careers.

Again, I think it's a big mistake to bank on a single idea or story or series. Or medium. Brian Bendis has pointed out that, no matter how popular a creator is, he or she usually has a shelf-life. I could point to several creators who were huge at one time, but who've virtually disappeared from comics now. I think we should all keep as many oars in the water as possible. If you're doing a company-owned book, you should also be doing a creator-owned book. Besides, I'm a big proponent of creator-owned books; that's where this industry gets fresh ideas, new talent and passion. If you're writing comics, you should also be writing novels or short stories or plays or films. Or all of those.

But I don't think you should abandon one medium for another. If you're trying to break into comics, you should be doing it because you love comics, not because you think it'll be easy. It's not. Comics shouldn't be a stepping-stone to another medium.

If you are lucky enough to break into comics and make a name for yourself, it's important to remember that somebody's reading what you've written. You owe that readership your best work, every single time.

When it comes to aspiring professionals, the biggest mistake I think you can make is to give up. You're going to be rejected again and again. Even after you break in, you're going to get some rejection. Develop a thick skin and keep moving. Writers are like sharks. You have to keep swimming or you'll die. So send that rejected pitch somewhere else and write a brand new pitch for the contact who just rejected you. Stay on the radar. If you have talent, the only reason you won't break in is if you give up.

COMICS CAREER: It's time to get philosophical: How would you sum up the most important "big idea" that you've learned in life?

GRECIAN: This is a tough one. Maybe it's this: empathize. If you can put yourself in other people's shoes, you'll obviously be a better writer, but I think you'll be better at everything else, too. If you can get inside your boss's head, you'll have a better idea of what he wants and how to give it to him. If you can see things from your wife's perspective, you'll be a better husband to her. If you somehow grasp what your toddler needs, you'll be able to communicate with him and head off tantrums before they happen. By empathizing with others, you can become a better person yourself. And you can create more well-rounded characters too!

COMICS CAREER: That's a great point. Thank you, Alex. I look forward to seeing what you have coming up next.

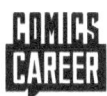

COMICS CAREER

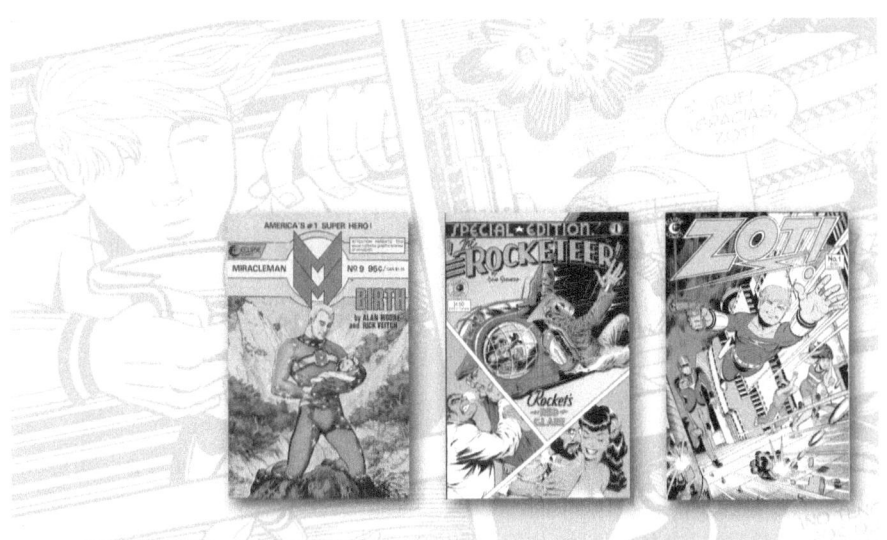

Cat Yronwode

Please indulge me as I tell the long story of how I met Cat Yronwode, the influential editor-in-chief of Eclipse Comics and eccentric character who changed my life by introducing me to comics fandom.

I was just 15 years old. She was still a few years from working with Eclipse. My buddies and I learned that there was a local club of adult comics fans near my southern Missouri hometown. We connected with the group's leader—a guy named Chris Rock (but not that Chris Rock)— through the mail. He invited us to a meeting.

We were given directions, and my friend's dad drove us. We headed out of town on a two-line highway, which turned off onto a county road, which led to a gravel road through the dense forest, which slowly degraded into a dirt path that crossed a stream with no bridge, which soon was only a pair of grassy ruts that finally led to a clearing on a hilltop with a log cabin in a field tended by goats. As we entered, we saw a lone poster on the wall: "The Poisonous Snakes of Missouri."

To be fair, I don't think Cat lived in this house, but she fit right in with 1960s hippie holdouts vibe. We met Chris Rock (still not that one), Cat, and several other club members.

Cat was the most dynamic personality of the evening, educating, enter-taining, and challenging a trio of pimple-faced adolescents. At the time, she was writing a small press review column in the weekly adzine The Buyer's Guide for Comics Fandom *(later known as* Comics Buyer's Guide*). As a result, she was giving away a boatload of review copies of small press comics fanzines. Those were the first amateur comics I'd ever seen.*

I'm sure it's impossible for younger people in today's Internet-driven, comics-saturated pop culture to understand, but my friends and I had had almost no interaction with other comics fans, let alone exposure to organized fandom. We had already been creating our own fan comics, but Cat's zines introduced us to a fascinating new world.

Those freebies led my buddies and me to create more fan comics, connect with other zine publishers, and—eventually—prompted my first profes-sional comics gigs. It also led to the creation of Comics Career Newslet-ter *itself. By then, Cat was editing the Eclipse Comics line and agreed to several* Comics Career *interviews.*

*Cat was generous with her time and wisdom. She had an eye for comics that combined quality and commercial appeal. Under her supervision, Eclipse built an impressive line of titles from top-level talent includ-ing Neil Gaiman (*MiracleMan*), Dave Stevens (*The Rocketeer*), Scott McCloud (*Zot!*), and P. Craig Russell (*The Magic Flute*). In this interview, Cat explores some of the disastrous ways that hopeful new creators bun-gled their attempts to sell their work to Eclipse.*

COMICS CAREER: What's the biggest problems of mailing in submissions to comics companies? Should people just avoid it entirely and find other ways of getting work?

YRONWODE: I don't want to be discouraging, because we have hired people based on their mail submissions, but I don't feel that even half the submissions we get are of even near professional quality. I would caution people against two things: sending in submissions when they can't truly believe their work is as good as what they see printed, and also getting an ego attitude that simply because they like comics, their work deserves to be in print.

For instance, [Eclipse Comics editor] Letitia [Glazer] got a call just a few days ago that was the most gutsy, and—how do I say it—obnoxious call. This man said he had created some characters and he wanted us to publish them. He had no interest in writing them; he just had them and was going to sell them to us.

We said, "That's very nice, but we have lots of characters already, and we have lots of good writers who'll create and write them for us." He just didn't understand. Creating characters is not the problem. Getting good writers and artists is the problem.

COMICS CAREER: I understand that editors are constantly surprised by new levels of rudeness—or at least a complete misunderstanding of the comics industry.

YRONWODE: One thing that we received recently that was a first was a batch of art—these were not professionally prepared pages. Not only was the art not professional, but the pages themselves had been colored with crayon or colored pencil—and they also sent in very primitive four color separations for a cover and the negatives, and a contract that they wanted us to sign. In the contract, we were supposed to promise them that we would pay them $71.72 per page; the material was what an educated child might produce. It was a gutsy thing to do, but entirely unprofessional.

So, I think that people out there really need some help. We've had a number of people through the years who have sent in submissions and get upset when they're rejected and say, but I went to art school."

That's very nice, but going to art school doesn't necessarily mean you're a good artist. They write back to us saying, "But I'm really good." One guy said, "Who died and left you God?"

Nobody did. I'm an editor and I just didn't want to use that work, you know?

We've been getting a lot of these attitude problem people. I noticed in your interview with Mark Gruenwald that he said something similar, and it's strange. The truth is, even if an amateur's very good, it's still extremely unlikely that they'll be put on a lead feature or the character that they've liked since they were seven years old because someone else probably has a contract on that character. Those things often go on a seniority basis or in terms of who's most popular in the direct sales market right now. An amateur can't just break in and get that character—and so many of them expect that.

I just have to say over and over again, no matter how good a person is, it's very likely that the first jobs they will be offered will be back-up jobs or fill-in jobs or helping someone else or finishing breakdowns by someone else, and they have to be prepared for that.

COMICS CAREER: Do you get many submissions that are really good?

YRONWODE: We've been getting some very good submissions lately. Within the last four months, we got one submission through the mail that was excellent and I have added to the list of people that I want to use eventually, if some of other company doesn't grab him first. In a way, I almost hope someone does, because he's so good I don't want him to have to hang around waiting for me. Whoever needs him first will get him, and he is good. He will become a well-known professional. I'm sure of it.

COMICS CAREER: Even though you're that sure, isn't there some way a person like that could still screw up?

YRONWODE: I have no idea what his deadline capabilities are, and I've found that too many times I'll take a chance on somebody who's a good renderer and I find that they can't meet deadlines at all. Later I laugh up my sleeve when, on the basis of what they've done for Eclipse, that person is hired away to go to DC or Marvel. I watch them mess up deadlines there too, and the next thing you know, they're out of the business.

There's a kind of weeding out process. Even if you're a good artist, there's a weeding out process of "can you meet deadlines" and "can you keep your temper?"

COMICS CAREER: What do people do wrong over and over in mail submissions?

YRONWODE: Again, I just have to urge people, *do not send original art*. Please print that in block caps; make a pull-out quote of it. It's just torturous to see these people send original art with no self-addressed, stamped return envelope. After a while, your patience wears thin.

I'm not Mike Friedrich. Mike used to have a comics company called Star*Reach back in the '70s. He used to print a notice saying submissions are not encouraged, all those without a self-addressed, stamped envelope will be trashed. [Laughs] That was printed in all his comics. I remember reading that and thinking, "God, there's a guy who's angry at the world."

We're not on that level.

COMICS CAREER: Joe Orlando told me that DC has a stack of 50 pages of original art with no return address that no one has the heart to throw away.

YRONWODE: We've had that happen too, and we've really lost some good prospects because of that. One time a guy turned in some beautiful stuff on speculation, and there was no address on it. It was lovely, and we were very interested in it. We showed it around to some other people, and eventually another publisher picked it up because he had sent them his address, and we didn't get it because we kept saying, "I wonder who this guy is?"

COMICS CAREER: Does a good mail submission get passed around so all the editors have a chance to see it?

YRONWODE: Oh, yes, exactly. That's precisely what we do. "Take a look at this artwork. This is the guy's name. Remember this if you need any art like that."

COMICS CAREER: I know you've got to go. Thank you for talking with me today!

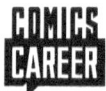

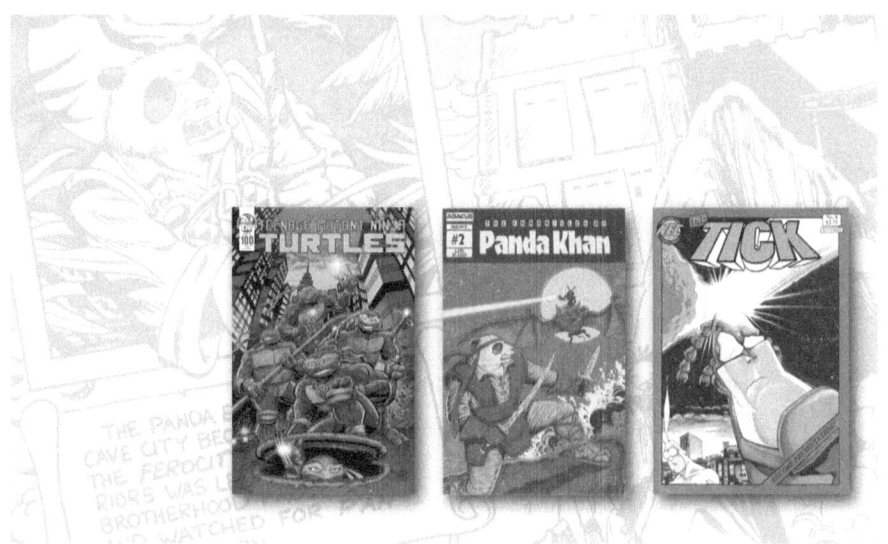

Dave Garcia and Monica Sharp

Dave Garcia and Monica Sharp are terrific examples of how talented creators can make connections, grow their skills, and parlay that into on-going work on creator-owned and work-for-hire projects. Garcia not only became a Teenage Mutant Ninja Turtles *artist, but thanks to their friendship with Peter Laird their self-published character* Panda Khan *was released as an early TMNT action figure.*

I interviewed Dave and Monica by phone in 1990. At this point, I had known them for several years. We met creating small press comics, and I included one of Dave's stories in my zine Plasma—*an issue which also featured a cover by pre-Turtles Peter Laird. Connections were made, and the rest is history, I suppose.*

COMICS CAREER: How did you get started in comics?

GARCIA: I got involved in comics by reading them when I was little. It just seemed like a natural progression. As far as publishing, that was Monica's idea.

I've done a lot of fanzines, but I don't consider those publishing. It's not on the same scale as what we've tried to do with *Panda Khan*. On my fanzines, I did everything myself, including the printing. It's not like scraping money together and going to a professional printer, giving them all this money, and expecting them to do everything.

COMICS CAREER: You got involved in fanzines and the fan network. Did that come about from those fanzines?

GARCIA: That was a little later. Monica's primarily responsible for that because she's a letterhack, and she wrote to a lot of people while I just sat around and drew. So, it was sort of a team effort. We've been a team for quite a while.

COMICS CAREER: You were a member of InterFan, right? [InterFan was an organization of aspiring comics creators.]

SHARP: He got into InterFan, but that was later. The thing that introduced us to the whole fan network was an issue of *Starlog* that listed a lot of fan organizations, and I started writing to them. We didn't know anything about mini-comics or fanzines or anything until later.

GARCIA: We'd been fans for a long time, but we'd just never known about fanzines and stuff like that.

COMICS CAREER: *Panda Khan* was originally created for the fanzines, right?

GARCIA: That's where it saw print first.

SHARP: *The Grape Press*.

COMICS CAREER: I thought Richard Harris' *Grape Press* was probably the first place to publish *Panda Khan*.

GARCIA: He was the first person to say, "Hey, I'll print that!"

COMICS CAREER: And then from there, you submitted it to WaRP and got it in as a back-up in *A Distant Star*?

SHARP: Not that directly. We went to the San Diego Comicon, and we were showing *Panda Khan* around to publishers. We met people from Comico back when they published, I think, three black and white books. They expressed an interest in it, and we talked with them for about a year.

GARCIA: I did a 20-page *Panda Khan* story that was going to go into *Comico Primer*. They advertised it and had my cover painting in their office for four months.

COMICS CAREER: And it was never published?

GARCIA: It never came about.

SHARP: We showed it to WaRP, and they liked it. That was around Christmas time of '83. We signed a contract with them in April of 1984, and it started coming out as a back-up in *A Distant Soil*. They had asked us what we wanted: to do a book or a back-up or what. We decided to do a back-up because at the time Dave was working full-time, and we didn't think we could meet even a bimonthly schedule. And you can see with our own publishing, we have a little trouble coming out every three months.

COMICS CAREER: That's something that a self-publisher is going to have problems with. To be commercial, you've got to appear regularly. Do you see that as being a drawback for you?

SHARP: Oh, definitely. If we're not coming out regularly, I think people forget that we ever did come out. We don't do enough advertising. We need more promotion, but we just can't afford it on the scale that we'd like.

SHARP: We didn't start self-publishing back when people were selling 50,000 copies of whatever and there were so many black-and-whites by people you'd never heard of before, and work that had never been seen. We came in when retailers were getting more cautious about what they were ordering. Our first order was about 10,000. Number two was 15,000. Number three was 8,000, and number four around 3,500. That's a significant drop, but it still paid for itself.

COMICS CAREER: But it wasn't very profitable.

SHARP: No. But Dave is working on the *Turtles*, so the money we live on is not coming from *Panda Khan*. It's something that we enjoy, that we believe in.

COMICS CAREER: If somebody is going to self-publish, would you encourage them to do it for the enjoyment rather than to make money?

SHARP: Well, at this point, if they're doing it in black and white and it's not a superhero, they'd better be doing it because they like it and not because they think they're going to get rich. Of course, you can never tell when you'll get a cult hit like *Flaming Carrot*.

COMICS CAREER: How did you learn how the distributor system works?

SHARP: Basically, we contacted the distributors. We did ask Peter Laird and Kevin Eastman. It was in your *Plasma* that we met Peter Laird, and he's always been helpful with advice and recommending printers and that sort of thing. But I couldn't bother him all the time, so basically, I called the distributors and they told me how things worked. I talked to other self-publishers to see what their discounts were and stuff like that. It's pretty much an industry standard of 60% for non-returnable books.

COMICS CAREER: Did you run into bad distributors?

SHARP: Yeah, there was a guy who really hurt us with #2. He was starting up a new mail order company on the east coast. He'd bought up our remaining copies of #1, paying C.O.D. He put in a big order for #2, at the same time wanting an exclusive portfolio/reissue of #1, with four different packages of the reissue, each containing artwork of a different character from the book. He contacted us in May and wanted the artwork the next month. Dave was busy on #2, which we wanted out before the summer cons got going, and we were leery of the portfolio deal—it sounded like a typical "scam the fans with instant collectibles." We finally said no, and when we shipped his C.O.D. order for #2, he refused shipment and moved. We got stuck with 5,000 issues that had no real market.

COMICS CAREER: Let's backtrack a bit and talk about how *Panda Khan* developed. Where did the original idea come from?

GARCIA: From an oil painting I did. Originally, years earlier, I'd done a realistic panda in watercolors. Monica said she wanted it, but as a starving college student, I sold it to someone. So, I owed her another panda, but I don't really enjoy painting nature scenes. I like science fiction and fantasy art, so, of course, the next panda I did was a fantasy panda with Asian garb, holding a traditional martial arts weapon, a kendo staff. I gave it to her, but I'd been thinking as I painted, "This is a neat character. I should make a comic strip about him," and that's how *Panda Khan* was born. The painting is on the cover of #1.

Our basic concept was, instead of making a typical talking animal comic, where there is no reason why they are *talking* animals, we'd have a reason why animals speak and have a human-like civilization.

SHARP: Since Dave and I are big nature lovers and environmentalists, we follow the research that's being done with Koko the gorilla and the other primates that have learned sign language. Even now, there's still a big debate whether it's truly communication or if they're just like Pavlov's dog and have just been trained to respond without truly understanding the meaning. We believe it is clearly communication and that other animals, like dolphins, do communicate on a level as sophisticated as ours—only humans can't understand it.

COMICS CAREER: It's a language, not just grunts and groans.

SHARP: Right. Although we can't understand it, they're obviously using some sort of sophisticated communication. Just because humans don't understand the animals' forms of communication doesn't mean that humans are naturally superior and more important. So, we place the story in the future and experimentation has been done on pandas. The future earth that we created is pretty much environmentally destroyed. People can't live on the surface.

GARCIA: Like we're headed now.

SHARP: So, they've colonized other planets and populated them. A lot of the science fiction that we read goes into *Panda Khan*. In science fiction they're always transforming planets to make them more Earth-like to live on, and that's what they've done in our story. They populate the colony worlds with Earth creatures, and a scientist tries to expand the sign language research to pandas.

So, he's doing his research and genetically alters the pandas so that they're able to speak. The government orders the scientific compound on this planet to be abandoned, so the pandas are left on their own, except for a computer which is self-aware. It goes crazy from all the years alone and goes beyond what it was supposed to do in protecting the pandas. It comes up with a mythology for them and has their human creator, the scientist, as a god and itself as a lesser god.

COMICS CAREER: So, it is a science fiction and fantasy. It's not *Donald Duck*.

SHARP: No, it's not *Donald Duck*, but we do enjoy *Donald Duck*.

GARCIA: It's more like *Uncle Scrooge*.

COMICS CAREER: That's a good point, because *Uncle Scrooge* was more along the lines of adventure stories and character interaction.

SHARP: Right. And we love that stuff. We bought all the Gladstone reprint books. We don't have anything against funny animals at all. It's just that we didn't go that way with *Panda Khan*. Although now we're working with Phil Yeh, and we're doing little short stories for him that are a lot more like Donald and his nephews getting into trouble than the regular *Panda Khan* stories are.

COMICS CAREER: Where are those seeing print?

SHARP: In his literacy comic called *Patrick Rabbit*. It's aimed at elementary school children.

COMICS CAREER: You knew that *Panda Khan* had an audience since WaRP had published it and other publishers were interested. How do you suggest that new self-publishers get an idea of how commercial their projects are?

SHARP: I think the best idea you get about how commercial your project is from the response you get from distributors. They all ask for artwork. If you're new in the field and they don't know you, they want to see the complete books, the response you get from the retailers and distributors will give you an idea of how commercial it is. If you don't get many orders for it, don't do it.

COMICS CAREER: What are some of the mistakes you can make that cause you to lose money?

GARCIA: I think our only real mistake is not putting the book out often enough. It's not been a mistake; it's just economics. We've *had* to do other things.

SHARP: When it's just two people, it's hard. Look at the *Turtles*. They have a whole staff of people who work with them, but when it's just Dave who does all the paste-up and layout and letters it and puts on the zip and everything, it's really a time-consuming process.

COMICS CAREER: And of course, they have the benefit of having created the black-and-white market and getting the full results of the booming market. [And, of course, since this interview, they've gone onto further success in TV and movies.]

GARCIA: They're a whole different ballgame.

COMICS CAREER: Do you think it's possible that somebody can recreate that excitement using the publicity techniques Kevin and Peter did?

SHARP: It's possible.

GARCIA: There's always something new that's hot. There's got to be somebody out there right now who's thinking of the next thing.

COMICS CAREER: How has this helped your careers? Monica, you substitute teach, right?

SHARP: Yes

COMICS CAREER: And Dave, you still do outside commercial art?

GARCIA: Yes, but less and less now.

COMICS CAREER: But as far as comics career beyond *Panda Khan*, Monica, do you have plans to do outside writing on projects without Dave?

SHARP: If I do other projects, they'll probably be with Dave. I've talked to a few people. Dave's an artist and we know more artists than writers. Sometimes an artist asks me if I want to do a project, but usually I say no. I feel like a rare being in comics because I'm a woman. *Panda Khan's* not a highly successful book, but we've never lost money. The longer we keep putting it out, the more our reputation grows as having a consistent project, even though we can't meet a deadline. When *Panda Khan* does come out, you may not care for the story, but at least it's intelligently written. And it looks great!

COMICS CAREER: Do you do all the writing on the strip?

SHARP: I do the writing, but we always sit around and brainstorm together, and sometimes when I give the plot to Dave, he'll do the layouts and there'll be something new in there. Dave is a lot funnier than I am on paper. He's always adding slapstick and funny bits.

COMICS CAREER: Do you think having a woman's point-of-view has helped *Panda Khan* stand out from other things on the market?

SHARP: I don't know. I get 15-year-old boys telling me at cons, "Oh, it's great, a woman writing stuff like this." But they're still spending money on superheroes.

GARCIA: It's helped us stand out. I don't know if it's helped make *Panda Khan* a success though.

SHARP: If we'd done *Panda Khan* as "Killer Claws," it probably would've sold lots more copies. We're not exactly aiming for the mass market of comics readers, which is teenage boys.

I've noticed frequently, although I'm Dave's manager and I handle the business side, other pros and even some of the newszines don't want to talk to me on the phone. I'm just "Dave's wife," so obviously I don't know anything.

My theory is that it's because comics are targeted to boys. Then the boys grow up and become pros. They're *men* now, but they're doing the stuff they liked as *boys*, which often excluded real girls. I don't know if I've just run into atypical artists, but a lot of the ones I've met aren't comfortable around women. Maybe it's me. But anyway, I think comics shouldn't be addressed to one sex, one age. You need to appeal to women as well. Heck, we outnumber men! And girls read more often than boys.

COMICS CAREER: Has *Panda Khan* been a big help to your career Dave?

GARCIA: *Panda Khan* was my ticket into other companies. No question about it. I'd been submitting things all over the place, but until we created *Panda Khan* the response was lukewarm.

SHARP: We submitted *Panda Khan* to Capital Comics which attracted Mike Baron's attention. He wrote to Dave.

GARCIA: I got to be in the first *Anything Goes* for Fantagraphics because Mike Baron sent me his story. I thought it was really neat. I'm in *Anything Goes* along side Gil Kane and Bob Burden and Alex Toth. All those cool dudes and me, a little nobody. I also did a couple of *Clonezones* with Mike.

COMICS CAREER: What other assignments have you picked up?

GARCIA: I've done a lot of inking: the first four issues of *The Trouble with Girls*, as well as other stuff for Malibu. I inked for Now Comics and *Cutey Bunny* and *Aunt Vicky* for Joshua Quagmire. I inked a Quagmire story in *Critters* #1. Inked one issue of *Man-Frog*. Right now, I'm inking

The Tick for New England Comics, my third issue with them. I've been inking Archie's *Turtles* books. I've been penciling and inking my stuff for Revolutionary Comics. I just penciled an issue of *Laugh* for Archie Comics.

I'm also doing some covers. I did the cover of that *Laugh* issue. And one for MU Press. The publisher, Edd Vick, is a guy I knew from fanzines. Another cover was for *Blue Comet*, which is another self-publisher's company.

COMICS CAREER: You got these assignments just because you got your work out there?

GARCIA: Some of it, yes. I send out samples, but most of the jobs I've gotten have been when someone contacts me because they're familiar with *Panda Khan*,

COMICS CAREER: Have you had a lot of success laying the groundwork for deals at conventions?

GARCIA: Yes and no. Conventions are good for touching base with folks. If you can make it to the big one, definitely go.

SHARP: Corresponding with other artists is good. Drawing is a solitary business, and you need the feedback. Plus, you get tips and inside information: who is good to work for, who to watch out for. At conventions, we've gotten to meet the people with whom we've been corresponding and talking with on the phone. People like Sam Kieth, who was in InterFan with Dave, and Joshua Quagmire, and Evan Dorkin. Even Mike Baron, we met at San Diego after writing and talking back and forth for about two years. Peter Laird, too. And John Holland, who was in InterFan, too.

COMICS CAREER: Really? I'd assumed that you'd met him through Gene

Frye, where David and I met. Or at least through my fanzine *Plasma*, which both of you and he were submitting to.

SHARP: Through Gene Frye we met you, and from *Plasma*, Dave went on to *Tyro*, InterFan's zine, and then on to places like Comico, almost, and WaRP. Fandom was a springboard. A lot of fannish artists and writers are now working pros.

GARCIA: I wouldn't be working on the Archie *Turtles* series if it wasn't for the fanzines, because that's how we hooked up with Peter Laird. He did the cover for your zine, didn't he?

COMICS CAREER: Yeah, *Plasma* #1.

GARCIA: After that, we started writing to Peter. That was before *Turtles* got big. We developed a friendship and finally met a couple of years later. That landed me the job of working on their Turtles book for Archie.

COMICS CAREER: Were you contacted by Mirage to do that, or by somebody at Archie?

SHARP: Peter called Dave and asked him if he'd be interested in inking the mini-series. Since our friendship predated them hitting it big, I had always teased Peter about how he should subsidize our family life; he could afford it. So, when the Archie deal came up, he called. Then after the mini-series was successful, but Michael Dooney wanted to go back to his own projects, they hired Ken Mitcheroney to replace Michael. But when Ken got tied up in his animation work, Peter called again and asked Dave to pencil and ink the first two issues of the new continuing series. Dave said, "Of course." Our son was really impressed. He loves the Turtles.

GARCIA: Then Kevin and Peter suggested to the toy company, Playmates

Toys, that they make an action figure of Panda Khan as part of the Turtle line. So, maybe if you go into your local K Mart today, you'll see Panda Khan right there next to Raphael and Mouser.

COMICS CAREER: Guys, this has been terrific. Thank you taking the time with us today. I'm looking forward to more cool stuff from you.

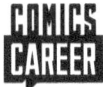

COMICS
CAREER

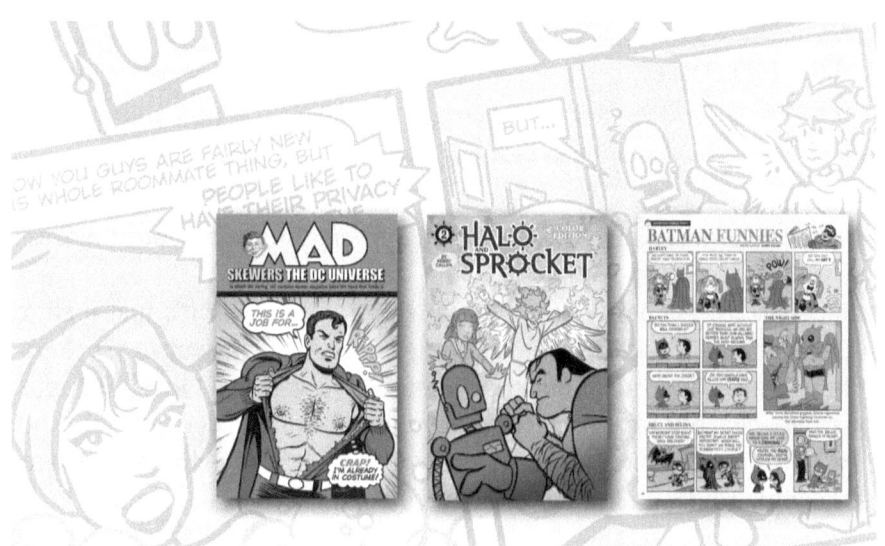

Kerry Callen

By day, Kerry Callen adapts the drawings of America's most popular cartoonists into greeting cards in Hallmark's licensing division. By night, he twists superhero conventions to create clever viral sensations and wickedly funny MAD *magazine parodies.*

At Hallmark, Callen mimics the work of renowned cartoonists, drawing famous comic strip characters in the poses or costumes needed for a particular greeting card. For example, Callen seems to channel the spirit of Charles Schulz from any point in his career — even replicating the wobbly ink lines of the Peanuts *creator's final years.*

Callen's graphic novel Halo and Sprocket *is a collection of stories originally published as a mini-series by SLG Publishing. It's nominally about a young woman (Katie) who lives with an angel (Halo) and a robot (Sprocket). In reality, it's an outlet for Callen's hilarious fascination with things that simply don't make sense when you think about them. No topic is too trivial to be turned into a mind-bending farce: burping, why there's no cursive version of numbers, and the fact that the proverbial glass is actually neither half full nor half empty.*

Comics Career *interviewed Kerry Callen at a comic book convention in*

2008 prior to his work at MAD *magazine.*

COMICS CAREER: Which of the *Halo and Sprocket* stories is your favorite?

KERRY CALLEN: Probably, let's look at the name of it... it's just a short 4-page story... You know what? Let me change my answer to "Suckers" where they're talking about spitting saliva. *[Laughter]* I like it the most writing-wise, but art-wise I wish I could go back and redraw it. I think it was the second story I drew even though it was printed in a later issue. But, it has the kind of dialogue I try to get in every story.

COMICS CAREER: Is that what's most important to you then, the dialogue?

CALLEN: Yeah, because all the *Halo and Sprocket* stuff is about the content more than the art. It's all about the writing because I'm an artist at my day job.

COMICS CAREER: How does the writing process work for you?

CALLEN: The writing part is easy because I have a 45-minute commute to work, so I have all that time to think about stories. They usually get pretty refined during the drive. It's the art that I usually have to rush through. Maybe that's why I feel better about the writing than the art.

COMICS CAREER: If you have the story pretty well worked out in your mind, do you skip straight to thumbnails then?

CALLEN: Since the dialogue is such an important part, I type it out and break it into sections: "that's worth about a page; that's worth about a page." Then I do little thumbnails. I have it pretty much broken down before I draw it.

COMICS CAREER: You mentioned your day job. Tell us more about that.

CALLEN: I work in licensing at Hallmark, which has been a good thing because over the years I've had the chance to meet Charles Schulz, Jim Davis, and people like that. Part of what makes it great is seeing that they are just real people—very talented people—but still just real people doing that stuff. At some point it occurred to me that maybe I'll try doing that, too. That's part of the reason I started doing *Halo and Sprocket* in the first place.

COMICS CAREER: I found the same thing when I got into comics professionally. The writers and artists are just people. They aren't demigods or anything. They're good at what they do. They have talent and the dedication to stick with it, but it's not that they're — I don't know — fictional or something.

CALLEN: (Laughs) Yeah, that's a good way to put it.

COMICS CAREER: What are the tools you can't work without — your essential creative tools?

CALLEN: Right now I work with pencil and brush and ink. One of my favorite parts of the process is inking with the brush. I'd like to train myself though to work on a Cintiq tablet or something where I work directly on the computer because it will cut my time in half. I enjoy the pencil and brush, but I don't want to say they're the tools I can't work without since I would like to work without them.

COMICS CAREER: What reference sources do you use frequently?

CALLEN: Well, most of this stuff is just based on my thinking time, driving to and from work. Occasionally, like in this latest volume, they go into a pet store and deal with a skink, which is a kind of lizard. So I had to look up lizards to find out what type I wanted to use. Then I had to do some research on skinks to find their bone structure and Latin name.

COMICS CAREER: So is Google where you go for something like that?

CALLEN: Absolutely. Oh, the internet is like magic. When I started, I had to go to the library for research. If I had to draw a bunch of cats—like I did on "Big Cat Puns"—I would have to go to the library and check out a big stack of books just to get a few images. But now with the internet, I spend five or ten minutes and find all the reference I need.

COMICS CAREER: What is it about the comics medium that appeals to you as a creator?

CALLEN: I think just the fact that you get to use words and pictures together. That's a pretty powerful combination. I guess the only thing more powerful would be film where you've got moving pictures and sound. But as far as what a single person can create, I think comics is more powerful than just pictures or just words.

COMICS CAREER: Who has had the biggest influence on your career and how have they had that influence?

CALLEN: Well, it kind of goes back to what I was saying before about being influenced by seeing that real people do this kind of thing. My first story I drew for the fun of it, just to see if I liked it, and I did. That's actually the first story in the first collection. So I drew a couple of more and sent them out to some publishers. That was just a shot in the dark to a few different places.

When I first started doing this, I wanted to do a single issue, like a 48-page special. I submitted that idea to places like Dark Horse, and they said, "Well, no we don't do just little short specials of stuff like that."

When I sent it to SLG, Dan Vado actually called me and asked if I would do a series. I told him I didn't have time to do a series and he said,

"Well, you can get a couple of issues done before we publish it." I said I still didn't know how much time it would take me and he just said, "We're very patient." Just him saying that to me helped a lot. It actually gave me permission to go ahead and do a series.

COMICS CAREER: Obviously you're involved in artwork during your day job as well. What are the things you do to continue to stretch and learn as a creator?

CALLEN: The great thing about working at Hallmark is that I'm around a lot of talented people. Just going there every day is a good experience for me. And everybody dabbles in different types of things, not just comics.

COMICS CAREER: Who are your closest confidants in the comics industry?

CALLEN: Well, Anna-Maria Cool I still talk to quite a bit. And Chris Grine who does *Chickenhare* for Dark Horse. Mike Huddleston who actually used to live here in Kansas City. He's drawing *Gen 13* now. We stay in touch pretty regularly. And also Rich Marcej who's dabbled in comics. Those are the people who, if I have an idea, I'll send it to them. It's like, "Here's my latest story."

COMICS CAREER: What's the biggest reward of creating comics?

CALLEN: It's always great when you finish a project and you like the product. But, sitting at a convention can be a lot of fun because if you boil it down, it's people coming by and telling you how great you are and giving you money. [Laughter]

COMICS CAREER: Yeah, that's pretty nice. Money and compliments.

CALLEN: It doesn't always happen, but...

COMICS CAREER: You said that the first time that you sat down to give comics a try, out came *Halo and Sprocket*. Was it fully-formed from the beginning?

CALLEN: That's the short version. The long version is that I knew that I liked comics and wanted to do something in comics. Well, aside from the few dabblings I'd done in the past. I wanted to do something where I could just throw out quirky ideas, and I was trying to decide how to do that. I considered an anthology book with different random stories, but working at Hallmark—and particularly working in licensing—I understand the power behind characters. If you read a *Peanuts* strip and it's not funny that day it's okay because you still like seeing Snoopy again. So, I think if you can create characters people like, it carries you through your weaker material.

So, I knew I needed characters. Then I started thinking, "What character could have quirky views of the world?" I just kept thinking of individual characters. Maybe a robot? But you've seen that a thousand times. Or an alien? But you've seen that a thousand times, too. Finally it occurred to me that I could have two different characters with quirky points-of-view. An angel and a robot gives me two opposite points-of-view on things: purely logical and purely metaphysical. Then, of course, I had to add a human just to have a real life point-of-view. Once that occurred to me that's when I went, well I'll just draw one of these up now. But I actually thought about it a while before I drew my first story.

COMICS CAREER: To me, the dynamic between these characters, logical and metaphysical, is really sharp. There seems to be magic in there. What are your thoughts about how that dynamic works.

CALLEN: Someone asked me the other day which character was me. I said, well, they're all me. That's the way people write. The only reason that Katie's a girl is just because I'd rather draw a girl over and over

106

than a guy.

So—thank you, by the way—but I don't see any magic in it. To me it's just getting thoughts that I've had on paper. To me everything's obvious. I think that's what creators do. They put what's obvious to them on paper. Not that there's not a lot of work involved in that sometimes.

COMICS CAREER: Well, I certainly like what you're doing! Thanks for talking with us today.

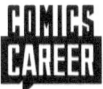

Mark Gruenwald

Mark Gruenwald arrived at Marvel Comics as an assistant editor and remained at the company the rest of his life. He did stints as editor of the Avengers, Captain America, Iron Man, *and* Thor. *He co-wrote the seminal mini-series* Marvel Super Hero Contest of Champions, *created the* Official Handbook of the Marvel Universe, *and a wrote a 60-issue run on* Quasar.

He became Marvel's executive editor in 1987. Among other duties, he was the official keeper of Marvel continuity.

This interview was conducted in early September 1988 by Kirk Chritton. It is a snapshot of the submission process at the time. Many things have changed, but this sums up the deluge of submissions that publishers can receive, and why they remain interested in looking for gems in the avalanche.

COMICS CAREER: What's the procedure at Marvel for submissions?

GRUENWALD: We have a submissions editor to handle the many submissions we get. I don't know how many other companies get, but I would say that it is no exaggeration that the submissions editor herself gets

100 pieces of art or writing samples per week. She cannot answer it quickly enough. There is always a backlog, and about twice a year we get all the assistant editors together to go through the backlog.

If the submissions editor finds anything that looks promising, we have this form memo that has all the editors names on it. She attaches the submission to the form memo and then it's passed up and down editorial row, and everyone whose office it goes into has to cross their name off to signify that they've seen it.

This has resulted in some people getting work, but it only gets passed around if they're in the ballpark. Otherwise, due to the volume, there are various form letters you'll get.

COMICS CAREER: About what percentage of the submissions actually get passed up editorial row?

GRUENWALD: She gets around a hundred a week, and I see maybe two or three a week, so two or three percent. Of course, you can send a submission to each of the individual editors. That's what you should do if it's a plot pertaining to one of the books, because only that editor can buy that plot. Only the Spider-Man editor can buy a Spider-Man plot. He'll just say, "Hey, this guy doesn't read the book." So, you should send plots directly to the editor. You can send art, but generally only someone who's already in the industry sends art directly to an editor whose books they like.

With the submissions editor, you will get a response provided you give an address not only on your letter, but also on the submission. A lot of people put their address on the envelope, but not on the letter, and not on the submission, and they get separated. That's going to happen. She gets 100 submissions a week, and there's no way to trace it. Some people are silly enough to send their original art instead of photocopies. Then if there's no return postage, we send them a letter saying, "Hey, do you want this stuff back? Then send postage."

So, the procedure is to submit photocopies of four or five pages of continuous storytelling if it's art, submit springboards for stories if it's writing. You can send it to the individual editors, but they each have their own policy on answering them. There are some people who always respond if you send return postage, and then there are some who I doubt have answered a single submission unless it was so great they couldn't pass it up.

I always answer my mail, but I can't hire much of anybody because I'm now executive editor and don't have a line of books anymore. If you send it to me and it's good and makes the cut, I'll send it up and down the row and send a response saying, "Yes, I got it. I'm not editing anything, so I can't hire you, but I'll show it to the other editors. If they have any work for you, they'll let you know."

So it's just a volume sort of thing, Send your stuff to the submissions editor and you're guaranteed a response eventually; send it to an editor with a line of books and you're taking your chances about getting a response. You can send it to Tom DeFalco and you'll generally get a response, but usually it'll be a form letter. I mean, he's not hiring anybody. He hires editors; the editors hire freelancers.

COMICS CAREER: When Jim Shooter was Marvel's editor-in-chief new talent seemed to be a high priority. Is it still as high a priority?

GRUENWALD: It's always a high priority. Jim liked to publicize that a lot. I don't think publicity makes that much difference in the volume or quality of the submissions we get. It makes good PR for us to say, "Yeah, were looking for new talent," but the fact remains that we only publish so many books and only need so many people to do them, and we try to get the best people we can to do them. That doesn't change. We've not increased or diminished our need for new talent even though we don't publicize it as much.

COMICS CAREER: What type of submission do you see too much of?

GRUENWALD: That's a good question. Personally, I see too many people who think they're going to break in with a multi-part saga, or with their own characters. That's just not the way it's done historically. I'm not saying there's any rule against it; it just doesn't work out that you come out of the blue and your first sale is something you've created. Or even worse, in Marvel's case, people take a bunch of our lesser known characters, put them together and give them a team name and claim they created them. Sorry, we don't want to publish a book like that right now. Y'know, in fact, it's already occurred to us to publish a book like that. Look at *The Champions*; look at *The Defenders*. There a reason we're not doing that anymore, but we still see a lot of it.

Newcomers shouldn't try to sell us a multi-part story. Most beginners work on inventory stories at first, and think about it—every inventory story you've ever seen has been a single-issue story. Epic Comics publishes creator-owned stuff, so they are looking for series, but think of how few completely new series Marvel has launched.

COMICS CAREER: That's true, most of Marvel's new books are spin-offs like *Excalibur* or *Punisher*.

GRUENWALD: Yes, let's see, *Speedball* is completely new.

I try to avoid reading new series proposals and character designs because the likelihood of us using it is astronomically low, and I don't want to be accused later on of appropriating someone else's ideas, and that could happen. There are only so many ideas, and occasionally we're going to create something similar to someone else's character.

There's a great case some years back in which we got a letter from an

Israeli saying that Sabra, a character which has appeared I think two or three times and is a woman from Israel, was just like his Sabra-Man which was kind of a Superman pastiche. Both characters' costumes were based on Israel's flag and had basically the same name. He claimed that we got the idea from him, although we'd never seen his self-publication. No, the fact is, a native-born Israeli is called a Sabra—you'll find it in the dictionary—and the costume was based on the flag.

COMICS CAREER: It sounds like a pretty obvious coincidence.

GRUENWALD: Yeah, so, we just tend not to look at new character designs or new series proposals, because that's not what we're looking for.

COMICS CAREER: Should artists try to match the Marvel house style?

GRUENWALD: I don't think Marvel has a house style. We don't tell Todd MacFarlane to draw like Sal Buscema on the Spider-Man books. As a result, Peter Parker doesn't look quite the same in one Spider-Man book as another.

COMICS CAREER: Mary Jane certainly doesn't look the same.

GRUENWALD: I think a house style would be more like Archie or Harvey Comics where they really want a character to look consistent. What we do have is a certain bare minimum standards of storytelling which is almost like a house style. Other publications, other publishers apparently don't tell people to make it clear and readable.

For the most part, Marvel comics tend to be readable and accessible. They're geared to the most basic level of comics reading. We don't want to trip people up in the structure. If there's something sophisticated, it should be in the material, not in the way the story is told.

From artists, we want to see four or five pages of continuity in sequence using Marvel characters. Either make it up or take a comic book that you don't think is particularly well done and try to draw it better.

COMICS CAREER: But, somebody who has a funny animal style would be better off submitting to Star Comics, and somebody with an avant-garde style should probably submit to Epic, right?

GRUENWALD: Yep. Or, I guess DC allows a lot more experimentation as far as storytelling.

COMICS CAREER: I know that you've done quite a bit of fanzine work in the past. Do you recommend that for aspiring writers and artists?

GRUENWALD: Definitely. Having work published and getting any sort of reaction is good. Thinking of my own fan work, only some of it applied to commercial work. In other words, after doing fanzines, I thought I knew a lot, and once I became a professional I realized it was very little. But at least I had an edge up on the people who had none.

When I was starting, I did some drawing and some people said, "I can't read this story. Which panel goes first?" I said, "Hmm, I guess I'm not doing my job well." So, I worked on improving.

COMICS CAREER: Is most of Marvel's lettering and coloring done by local talent?

GRUENWALD: Not really. We have quite a few people in California. It's easier when you're here. In the beginning how you get into it is if you can turn it around quickly and it's basically competent. The people who can turn it around fastest come in that day, pick it up, take it home and bring it back the next day. Mailing it adds at least two days to that, so it helps to be here first.

Let me ask you a question. How many issues have you done so far?

COMICS CAREER: I'm working on #5 right now.

GRUENWALD: Well, I guess I don't have all my back issues. I think your publication is great.

One thing I wish is that people had is a better sense of when they're close to being ready or when they're nowhere in the ballpark.

When we say we get drawings done in crayon and pin-ups traced from *Marvel Universe* with a letter saying, "When can I draw *the X-Men*? it's a slight exaggeration, but not by much.

If they would say, "I love the X-Men and here's my rendition. Please keep it with my regards," we'd say, "Hey, this is really nice. This person's been inspired by what we're doing and it's great that they've vented their creative juices this way." Instead, we usually get the attitude of, "I buy your comics all the time; you owe me a living in comics, and this is only how good I am. Fire John Byrne and give me a job."

It's that attitude that I find real strange. You know, I was out there, and I was very close to being ready before I dared show anyone my work.

If your publication can do anything at all to help people figure out when they're ready to start submitting, it will at least keep down the volume a little so that we can spend more time with people who are on the verge.

COMICS CAREER: That's really one of my goals. On one hand, I want to help my readers get better, but I also want to help the companies weed out some of the weak submissions. Hopefully, these people will read the newsletter, see that they've still got a lot of work ahead, and try to improve before they waste their time collecting rejection slips because they're just not ready yet. I know that I thought I was the greatest comics writer living when I was 14. Now I have the perspective to know better.

GRUENWALD: Yeah, I'd be the last person to tell someone, "Gee, you don't draw very well. Give it up." I never tell anyone that, because I draw for fun. No one can take that fun away from me. On the other hand, if they really expect to make a living at it—and for some of these people that's not very realistic—I don't want to dash their fantasies, but I want to help them out now so their fantasies don't get bigger and bigger and they fall harder.

I don't know how to do that. When I write a "Mark's Remarks" and try to say a few words about whether it's a realistic career goal for the vast majority, I get nothing but negative response. People say, "How dare you tell me I can't have this fantasy." They say, "You're mean, "You're elitist," "You're the type of guy who crawls to the top of the hill and kicks anybody who tries to get up there with you." That's not true. I'm just telling them that there's only so much room at the top of the hill, and I don't have to kick them for them not to be able to make it.

I'm actually just telling them to decide if this is really the hill they want to climb, or is it another one? Anything you can do in that regard can certainly help editors from all companies.

COMICS CAREER: Thank you for the kind words, Mark. And thanks for taking the time to talk with us.

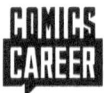

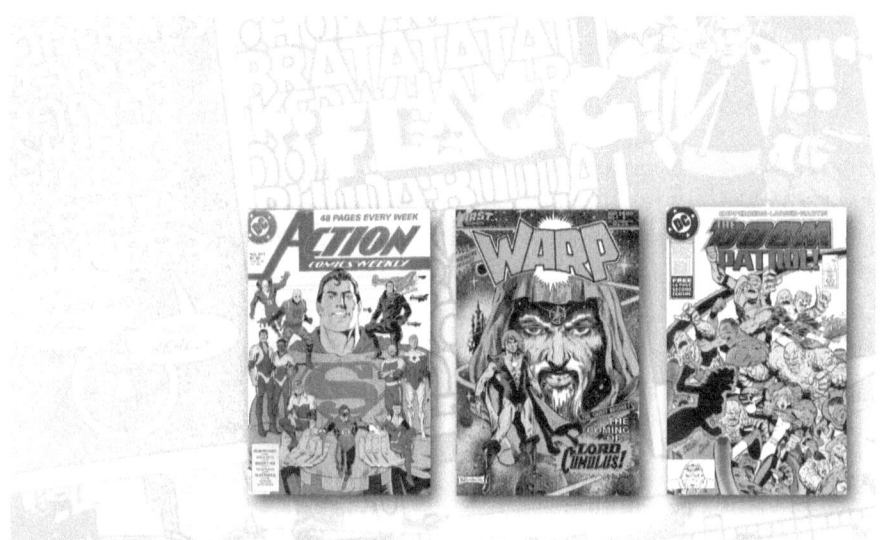

Mike Gold

Mike Gold is a multi-talented editor and executive who has succeeded in a wide variety of roles in diverse fields. As he tells in this interview, conducted in 1988, he came from the world of comics conventions, to comic book marketing, to the editorial side. He co-founded First Comics, then became director of editorial development at DC Comics. In that role he was a master at bringing creators together for exciting new projects.

COMICS CAREER: Do you have the opportunity to work with new talent often?

GOLD: All the time. One of the main reasons I go to conventions and do a lot store appearances is to look at people's portfolios. It's just that simple. I like to talk to people. It's nice to hear what they have to say about the comics we're doing. We get a lot of interesting ideas and we find out what people like and don't like. They're very vocal and that's wonderful, but I spend a lot of time looking at people's portfolios.

It's still hard to find an opportunity to talk to a would-be writer. It's very, very difficult, and I'm sure you've heard this over and over and over again. A convention is probably the worst possible setting to talk to a fledgling writer. I've said this before, and it sounds very unfortunate, but the easiest way to get an editor at DC to read your stuff as a writer is to try your hand at some of the smallest publishers first. You can experiment and make a lot of your early mistakes that way. More importantly, even if these guys don't pay very much or anything, it's a good opportunity for you to learn how to write visually, which the most difficult thing to teach. It's the Catch 22. You need the experience, but you're not going to get the experience unless you know how to do it.

There are a tremendous number of smaller publishers, very small publishers, and medium size publishers around. You can sort of work your way through that system. I'm not just talking about some of the better-known independent publishers; I'm talking about really small publishers. It's much easier for an editor to read a copy of a small black and white publication that may have only 200 copies out there than to read somebody's 40-page script. Nobody has the time to do that. It's unfortunate, but nobody has the time.

COMICS CAREER: An example of someone who came up through that system would be, well, Mike Baron. *Nexus* was originally a black and white at Capital Comics.

GOLD: That's right. Mike Baron got his start through Capital and then through First. John Ostrander got his start over at First, which is bigger than the smaller publishers, but still is a way to make it to DC or Marvel. Mark Verheiden got in at Dark Horse.

Now, I'm not saying that the pinnacle and be all and end all is to work for DC or Marvel. That certainly isn't true.

Still, I don't want to make it sound like you shouldn't be working for Dark Horse or some other smaller publishers. There's a tremendous amount of freedom and opportunity there. These are very valid outlets.

I think the attitude that newcomers should take in coming into the field is that they're getting into show business. I'm not saying that in the sense of vaudeville; I'm saying it in the sense of show business. You work for 20 years, and sit down and really perfect your craft and you rehearse and you audition and you go back and you improve and you audition. You audition for a number places. That type of thing. You know, that's really show business, what the system is all about.

I've never met a person, artist or writer, who came into the business and became the next hot name who hadn't been working at it for years and years and years beforehand. He may have started when he was eight! He may have started when he was eighteen or twenty-eight but he or she had been at it for a long, long time. He has to be tremendously patient in every way, shape, and form.

There's this breakthrough period for virtually every artist or writer where they're 95% there. They're within that last 5% of actually making it. They're at the point of actually being employable, and the needs of the publishers from time to time are so strong, that when you get within that last 5% you can get work. You can turn it into a living.

The problem is, once you start making those deadlines and putting your energies towards deadlines and doing it every month, every day, you're going to continue to learn, but now you'll learn at a much slower rate. You're busy acquiring these other skills. The skills of making a deadline, of getting along with your collaborators and editors. As writer you'll be learning just how the letterer is going to visually interpret your scripts. As a penciler you'll be learning how your art will get moved around if you didn't leave enough room for the copy, how the inker will interpret the pencils, what color is going to do to everything. How you write for color as well as draw for color. You know, there are those things that are really difficult to learn until you're really out there doing it.

That's the most important time for a newcomer to be patient. That last 5% can take you two weeks, it can take you six months, another year. But don't give in to that terrible itch of going in and turning professional before you're ready because there are an awful lot of newcomers who came in, looked hot, looked like they had a lot of potential, but never got any better and generally deteriorated pretty fast.

Some of these guys will disappear for a few years and then come back and be really good. I don't want to slam anybody here by saying this, but you can go back and look fifteen years ago, ten years ago, five years ago, and look at some of the back-up features or lesser books where you're likely to see new talent and see various people and wonder whatever happened to them. "Well, that guy disappeared for a couple of years." Those are the people who came in just before they were ready.

That's very critical. Once they're offering you work, be aware that you may not be ready for it yet. Get past your enthusiasm, get past the tremendous ego thrill of being offered work, and make sure that you've gone as far as you can go through the learning phase before you get into the doing-it-for-a-living phase. It's very, very important.

COMICS CAREER: How can developing creators get advice on how to proceed?

GOLD: If you want to get some feedback fast, you're going to have to make an investment in your career — a financial investment, not just time and energy. My recommendation is that you go to a convention where one of the editors is appearing, and talk to the editor there.

Smaller conventions are better. San Diego and Chicago are unbelievable. There are hundreds of guests and hundreds of dealers. There's a lot of business being done. For editors, those are really trade shows more than anything else. Smaller conventions, where they have 500 or

1,000 attendees, two or three guests, fifty or sixty dealers tables, that sort of thing, are a lot better for showing your work.

And if you're a convention promoter, and I speak as a former convention promoter, if you know that there are several would-be writers and artists in your area, it's a good idea to ask one of the editors from DC or Marvel or one of the other publishers to come down just to look at portfolios and talk to newcomers. It's a wonderful attraction for a convention promoter. A lot of inexperienced promoters tend to think that it's not a real attraction, yet as an editor, I really enjoy coming to these conventions to do exactly that. And, quite frankly, I come back to the same conventions every year or two to see how certain people are progressing.

I'm sort of a semi-regular here at Kansas City. This is probably the fourth convention I've been to here, and there are people that I've seen every time. I can see them progress. It's wonderful. There's one guy here, who I think has finally fallen within that 5% zone, which is the most difficult time, but at least he's gotten that far.

My main advice is to go to conventions if you can. I know that you're working and have things to do with your life and every spare moment is already devoted to perfecting your craft, but this is show business and the auditions don't come to you. You have to go to the auditions.

COMICS CAREER: What are the basic requirements that a writer or artist needs to have to break in?

GOLD: Well, being a Will Eisner clone helps—being ungodly talented.

You can see the person's work if they're an artist, and you know, you need to know all the things artists know they need: great anatomy, great storytelling abilities, you need a certain flash in your work. You need to have memorized Will's book [*Comics and Sequential Art*].

For a writer, you also need to have memorized Will's book. You also need to be able to tell stories visually and to appreciate the economy of words. The process for a writer is different if you're also an artist. That's why some of my favorite writers are artists — because they understand both sides of the fence. A writer has to learn the other side of the fence.

A writer also has to understand from an ego standpoint, that although the story originates with the writer, it's going to interpreted and told visually by the artist. There's a certain emotional maturity that's required from a writer in this job because they have to understand that the story is at the very least a collaborative effort and the primary responsibility for telling the story that the people will actually read is going to come from the artist's interpretation.

After that, patience, bathing frequently, any other interpersonal skills are helpful. You don't have to put on a suit and tie to go to one of these auditions. Not by any stretch of the imagination. Your work will speak for itself. But be polite because I'm going to see twenty people every day, and maybe a hundred people every day depending on how big the convention is, and I'm human too.

COMICS CAREER: Do first impressions play a large part in it?

GOLD: I think that's true to a degree in any human contact, but, no, not really a significant part. There's a line that you get all the time. I think you've written about it before. A kid'll come in—a kid meaning anyone who's not in the business, of course—a newcomer will come in and say, "Hey, I'm as good as that guy."

"Yeah, but that guy's awful!"

"Well, you give him work."

"Yeah, but he's 152 years old and we were desperate and we hired him once when we were drunk and he's helped us out of a jam and he can turn everything in overnight and sometimes that's really needed because we have to make our deadlines, but we're not really crazy about it. Don't tell me you're as good as the worst or even as good as the average. Show me you're unbelievably great—and can get better."

It's show business! It's an audition! We're dealing with potential when we're dealing with newcomers. We can see potential, but you're dealing with an awful lot of men and women who have just as much potential as you do. So, not only do you have to be better than all the people who are in the field, but you also have to be better than all those other hundreds and thousands of people who are in line with you.

COMICS CAREER: There's a lot of competition.

GOLD: There's a tremendous amount of competition. It's not a one-on-one competition. It's not a baseball game where you're playing them. You're competing with thousands of people.

It's a matter of only having so much work for so many people. We can still only publish so much material. Not just in terms of editors and writers and artists, but in terms of letterers and colorists and production personnel and color separators and printers' schedules and newsstand rack space and fans' attention span and pocket books.

The comic book field in general requires a tremendous financial commitment from a comic book reader. It's not that we want you to spend every penny that you have—although I imagine that there are business people involved in every publishing venture that would feel real comfortable with that—but the type of stories that are the most popular lead you to buy more comics. The whole fact that we deal with universes, The DC Universe, The Marvel Universe, The First Universe, The Eclipse Universe, contributes to that. The personalities also figure into that. You like Jim Starlin so you're going to read his work over here, here, and here, so that's already a ten dollar a month commitment and if you like three or four other guys you're spending a lot of money.

If you're coming in and you're talented as all hell, we really want to back your stuff 100%. In order to promote it fully, it's possible that it won't get into print for more than a year. There are certain technical reasons why that happens, but even once you have everything down, it takes six months just to produce a comic book. There are contractual negotiations. There's always going to be some changes in your concept. Even if it's just so beautiful that we want to publish it as is, we'll still spend a few months dealing with working relationships, contracts, and that type of thing. Then, we'll schedule it.

Patience is important, and you have to understand that when you're coming in. Chances are, no matter how good you are, you're not going to get work tomorrow. Those people who do are not only the exceptions, but they're the guys who win the lottery. "Oh, yeah, I won the $55 million, sure."

There's no malice on anybody's part. A good editor is going to understand that the man or woman standing before you with a portfolio or script—even if their stuff is terrible—really wants the shot and is working hard and believes in the concept. We're very impressed by that and understand the newcomer's position.

The opposite has to be true as well. In order to sell yourself and your work, you have to understand what the needs of the marketplace are and what the conditions of the marketplace are. It's very, very hard, and I have no sympathy for anybody who whines about it because everybody has gone through it no matter what position they've had in comics.

COMICS CAREER: How did you get in?

GOLD: They just walked up to me and offered me a lot of money. I was that guy with the lottery ticket. *[Laughter]*

I was probably one of the first people to get into comics through the convention side of things. I had been in media for eight years by the time Jenette [Kahn] offered me the job back in '76. So, I had a very good, solid background in media. For a short period of time I had been one of the people organizing the Chicago Comicon, and Jenette and I had a number of conversations on a variety of comics-related areas because of the preparation work for that show. She'd just become publisher at DC a couple of months after we had decided to do the first Comicon. I had known Jenette from my work in other media; she was publisher of a youth-oriented magazine, and I was an organizer of a runaway hotline program at the National Runaway Switchboard. I became friendly with one of her reporters and Jenette and I met that way. Stan Lee had agreed to be our guest of honor at the Comicon and I figured, "Well, Stan's publisher of Marvel, wouldn't it be interesting to get the new publisher of DC here?"

Jenette and I just started talking. We had these two-hour conversations three times a week for months and months and months. She then asked me if I'd be interested in coming out to New York to talk to Neal Adams about taking a coordination job over at Continuity Associates. I had known Neal from the *Warp* days when he was working on the Broadway version of that play. I had been very, very close to that cast and the theatre company throughout the one year run of *Warp* in Chicago and some of the earlier productions. I'd done work for that theatre and subsequently we did a comic book for them in 1980. I thought that would be interesting, although I was very happy with the work I was doing in Chicago and it was very involving. But, what the hell, I figured it would be fun to go out to New York and talk to Neal and Jenette.

What happened was, when I got to New York, some last minute problem forced Neal to cancel out on the lunch meeting. Jenette and I wound up talking face-to-face for four hours. The next day, I flew back to Chicago and Jenette called and said, "Forget about Neal, do you want to work for DC?"

The job was director of public relations, which was the first time that position had ever been developed in comics and was the first strictly marketing-related position other than simply dealing with the newsstand distributors. It was the first time that somebody was hired specifically to deal with the growing direct sales system. The job put me into very strong contact with the editorial aspect of comics. A lot of the input I had was editorial input, sort of a consultant editor. "Here's how you can make your books more accessible, more interesting to people who buy in the direct sales system."

It must have worked because in two years our direct sales circulation more than quadrupled. Some of that was the growth of the system, of course, but the whole market didn't quadruple. Our circulation quadrupled because we paid attention to it.

I left DC after two years, because, quite frankly, I took the job as a two-year job. I had commitments to the people I had left in Chicago. There was a video magazine which I had been offered the editorship of and was very interested in. I had missed the hands-on editing.

Through my work with the Comicon, and consulting work for several writers and artists and retailers I got the opportunities to create First Comics. That almost didn't happen. Rick Obidiah was trying to sell the comic book rights to *Warp* and I was his consultant on that. I told him up front that the best way to do that was to do it himself. Rick thought that was a ridiculous idea, until he started negotiating with Marvel and DC. Then he came back and said, "Yeah, you're right. Let's do it."

First is still going today, and I'm very happy about that. After five years with First, DC offered me the senior editor job, which developed into the director of development job, and that's why I'm sitting here talking to you today: I was born in a log cabin I helped my parents build.

COMICS CAREER: In other words, you got into the comics industry by already being a professional in another field and being qualified to come in editorially.

GOLD: Well, yes. I got involved in an editorial position in comics because I got the chance to prove my abilities in comics through my public relations work and marketing work. I'd gotten my marketing job because of my experience in the real world.

When I started out with the Comicon, the distinction between professionals and the fans who do fanzines and conventions was beginning to blur. For a long time, I've felt that a person who puts on a convention for a living or as part of their living and the people who run comic book shops or the people who do fanzines for a living are working comics professionals.

COMICS CAREER: For example, you can't say that Don and Maggie Thompson are only fans; they're professionals.

GOLD: They're professionals, absolutely. They do it 24 hours a day, seven days a week, 52 weeks a year and they never miss a week. No matter what the definition of the publication is itself, they're working professionals. No doubt about that. Gary Groth and Kim Thompson are working professionals and were long before Fantagraphics was doing a dozen different magazines and publications each month.

The service that you provide is a very professional service. It's a very needed service for everybody. It's the future of the industry. How else do you get people into the industry? Well, they either blunder their way in, or they get some guidance. One of the two. For fifty years we've primarily existed on people blundering their way in, or sort of perceptively figuring this stuff out. Now they have some guidance. That's terrific.

There's this fannish sense of wonder when someone sits down and says, "Wow, I really want to do this! I can do it!" If you're going to be doing the superhero comics that are geared to the 13 to 16-year-olds, it's important to be in touch with that part of yourself. In the beginning, that feeling runs away with you a little bit. That's okay; at a certain point you realize that to turn professional you have to have a professional attitude. But, there's nothing wrong with being enthusiastic. God, did you see me clawing over Dick Sprang in the con? I mean, come on! I'm 38 years old and going nuts!

COMICS CAREER: Me, too! Mike, I really appreciate your insights. Thanks so much.

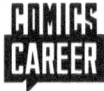

Index

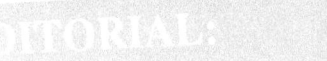
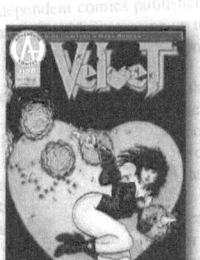
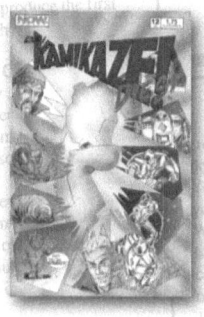
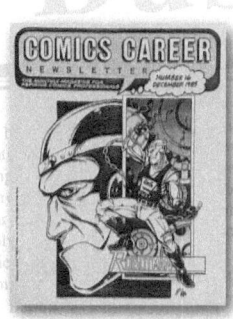

About the Author

Kirk Chritton founded *Comics Career Newsletter* in 1987, not long after his first professional comics writing assignment.

He started his own journey as a fanzine publisher, producing eight-issues of *Sharpshooter* with collaborators Robb Cox and Mark Runyan. He later assembled talents including Peter Laird and Dave Garcia for his anthology *Plasma*.

Chritton served as assistant editor for Jim Steranko's entertainment magazine *Prevue* and later contributed to industry news publications including *Comics Buyers' Guide* and *Comics Week*. He wrote *Dai Kamikaze!* for Now Comics and *Velvet* for Malibu Graphics' Adventure Comics imprint.

Comics Career Newsletter spanned 28 issues and included content specifically for aspiring comics writers and artists. Chritton eventually set the project aside after the birth of his children, and returned to it in an online version in 2008.

Today, he works in marketing for a large professional services firm. He and his wife live in Kansas City.

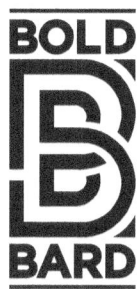

Bold Bard is dedicated to contributing fun and informative books and graphic novels to the world's collective library. We are a highly selective publisher, producing only a few projects each year.

Watch for more books dedicated to the craft of cartooning and comic books in the **Comics Career** library.

Find out more about our publications and submissions guidelines at BoldBard.com.